To Dad
30 April 1985
love Gra + Suz

ZED

ZAHEER ABBAS

Overleaf: Relaxed and happy: runs in the book.
(Photograph Patrick Eager)

ZED
ZAHEER ABBAS

ZAHEER ABBAS
with
DAVID FOOT

WORLD'S WORK LTD
The Windmill Press
Kingswood   Surrey

*To Najma and my daughters ;
to my parents and relatives at home ;
to all my friends in Pakistan and England.*

Text © 1983 Zaheer Abbas and David Foot
Published 1983 by
World's Work Ltd
The Windmill Press, Kingswood, Tadworth, Surrey
Filmset and printed in Great Britain by
BAS Printers Limited, Over Wallop, Hampshire

ISBN 0 437 05420 9

Contents

Acknowledgments

Zaheer's thanks go primarily to his family. He is grateful to his parents for their guidance and the influence they have had on his life: to his father, also, for memories of Zaheer's childhood, and to wife Najma for adding her warm and kindly impressions. There are many good friends at home in Pakistan who have generously encouraged the cricketer's outstanding Test career. He remembers, too, the friendships he formed and came to cherish in England. It saddens him that his 'White Daddy', Tom Hennessy, a former Gloucestershire C.C.C. committee member, who took a paternal interest in Zaheer when he arrived first in Bristol, died a few months before this book was published. Tom and Edna Hennessy had helped with reminiscences.

Zaheer thanks Bert Avery, the county scorer, for supplying elusive facts and illuminating insights as the book was being researched. Keith Ball, a former schoolmaster whose cricketing loyalties stretch from Bristol to Cardiff (and even occasionally Taunton) has once more demonstrated his invaluable zeal as a statistician.

David Graveney and the Gloucestershire players have weighed in with an anecdote or two; so have popular ex members of the side like David Shepherd and Jack Davey, while a perceptive assessment of Zaheer by another former county player, David Green adds to the texture of the portrait. Pakistan Test players have been equally cooperative, and especially Intikhab Alam who always found time to offer a comment or grant a facility.

Photographs were kindly provided by Patrick Eagar, Mark Foot and Zaheer's family.

Profile

Zed is a letter which has transformed and turned the alphabet in Karachi and Cheltenham on its head.

It is the phonetic symbol for Zaheer Abbas, whose peaks of consummate artistry have often made him look Pakistan's greatest batsman and at the same time a fugitive from another cricketing era: a shy prince who shimmers in his white silks.

Yet as a prince he eschews the trappings of the palace. The grandeur and the innate nobility are encapsulated in the strokes he plays. The only indulgence he allows himself as a concession to ostentation is an engagingly exaggerated flourish in the backlift. Even that has diminished in the pragmatic process of adapting to county cricket. The bewhiskered, with long and fond memories, say he belongs irrefutably to the Golden Age—along with Ranji, Trumper and the rest. And so, of course, he does.

I must declare a personal interest. From the first day he arrived at the county ground in Bristol in the early seventies, putting on three sweaters and then gazing at the unfamiliar surrounds of the grey Victorian orphanages before walking to the nets, I have spent an inordinate amount of time watching, admiring and writing about his batting. My reaction has reflected varying degrees of awe, adulation even, and occasional dismay.

Zaheer is not a garrulous person. He avoids parties, sponsors' tents and sycophantic supporters. As a high-ranking 'Syed', he has a natural sense of courtesy. The social status is evident—in the way he carries himself and behaves. One suspects that he doesn't always enjoy the more mundane, bread-and-butter

9

element of workaday professional cricket: irksome club disciplines, humping of kit and charting of distant motorways in the early hours of the morning. He prefers things to be done for him.

Like so many Pakistan players, he has extremes of temperament that those from the West are apt to find hard to understand. He is easygoing and stubborn, gentle and yet at times resentful. He's a man of inestimable good nature—and one who does not easily surrender a grudge. He warms to vast, appreciative crowds, his ears tingling with boyish excitement at the applause as an off-drive rattles against the fence; away from the field, he recoils from those who want to go on talking about the game. He retreats for a domestic curry and an evening watching television with his wife and the daughters he idolises.

As a psychological study, he's complex in the same way that Wally Hammond was. The comparison is not as tenuous as it may seem. Both saved their eloquence for the crease; both were withdrawn and defensive. Both engendered enormous respect and both opted for a privacy that did not come easily in a cricket dressing room. There, I would suggest, the comparison ends. Hammond could be surly and cruelly dismissive. Zed's personality is altogether sweeter.

Yet he, too, can brood. Batting, almost from boyhood, has been an obsession. He dreams of making runs. At home he fondles a bat as often as others pick up a knife and fork. He drives to the ground with his mind on square-cuts rather than pedestrian crossings.

Frank Twiselton, a former chairman of Gloucestershire, is in absolutely no doubt about Zed's car-driving ability. 'He's the worst I've ever known. Once he took me from the team hotel near Marble Arch to the Oval. I've never been so terrified in all my life. He drove very slowly—but his head was everywhere!' The story is told with affection.

In the course of this book I have talked to scores of people who know Zaheer—relatives, friends, team-mates, supporters. Not once did I detect a malicious thought. Almost without exception they expressed a sense of privilege that they had seen him bat. Players called him deep rather than devious. They said they might never get to know him, any better than the first day he turned up, but they all liked him.

There were reservations. One young, perceptive team-mate at Bristol told me: 'I'm never quite sure what to make of him. There are days when he looks as though he simply isn't interested. We watch the way he walks to the wicket with an air almost of indifference. But he's fooled us again. Once he takes guard, all the application is there again.'

His all-embracing love of scoring runs leaves him open to criticism that he can be a somewhat selfish team-man. It is a fair argument but isn't borne out by the evidence. He believes that centuries win matches. His performance probably takes priority in his mind over that of the team's success in the short-term. But I'm yet to be convinced that this attitude is unusual in professional sport.

A batting partner, unfortunately run out, has been known to throw a momentary look of protest down the length of the pitch. Others have perhaps contemplated the supposed imminence of a heart condition. I am thinking of David Shepherd, rotund cavalier of Gloucestershire until the days he turned to umpiring. In the first round of the Gillette Cup in 1976, Worcestershire came to Bristol. Norman Gifford won the toss and put Gloucestershire in on a perfect wicket. In no time at all, Sadiq and Stovold were out; then came a 95-run stand between Zaheer and Procter. Zed went on to score 128 and win the Man of the Match award.

I watched every ball and was absorbed by one partnership— Zaheer and Shepherd. It contained every emotion known to man. It bubbled with high comedy; it threatened to border on Greek tragedy.

Shepherd was in many ways the ungainly darling of the Bristol crowd. They loved his whims and superstitions; his delicious Devon-cream humour and his tribal postures whenever the score teetered on 111. They also loved his size. He put on weight every winter—and then, with huffing and puffing in the early season training routines, he ritualistically shed at least a couple of pounds at the most, it seemed. In the dressing room, he pulled at his battered pipe, stuffed with Clan tobacco and

With Najma—
at home in Karachi.

Domestic happiness.

The intimate family circle: parents, wife and children.

talked of days back in north Devon where, he alleged to the disbelieving, he was the most nimble scrum-half on the village rugby circuit. In truth, whatever the generosity of his girth, he moved well on the cricket field and could judge a sharp single better than most.

There were, alas, a great many sharp singles against Worcestershire in that Gillette Cup fixture. Zed kept calling for them—and Shep obliged. It was a matter of hilarious, sadistic pleasure for the spectators. Gifford was flummoxed, waiting to place a defensive field and yet reluctant to let this adventurous Pakistani and rosy-faced Devonian continue their audacious orgy of singles.

So it went on. Shep, remorselessly called by Zaheer, sprinted from one end to the other. By this time his shirt was out and the peak of his cap was over his right ear. He was mopping his bronzed brow between every delivery. His colour had heightened still more. I was standing near Mike Procter whose emotions were transfixed somewhere between team pride and mirth. 'Bloody hell!' was the collective team comment.

Suddenly there was a hush. Shepherd (39) was in need of attention. He was on the point of collapse. He muttered something and the close fielders ran forward. There was a long delay and then he was gently helped from the field. No-one was laughing any longer. He was guided to the treatment room and laid on the table. Physiotherapist Les Bardsley was there with smelling salts and soothing words. Half an hour later I tiptoed in. Shep was still stretched out, still perspring, still speechless. The South Molton twinkle was missing for once. 'He'll live,' said Les, with the customary black humour of the treatment room.

It was later relayed to the press box that David Shepherd was suffering from an acute attack of sun-stroke. I daresay he had his own theories. But as far as I know he bore Zed no grudge; they remained warm friends and were known to exchange wry words, laced with grins. Shep looked on it as exhaustion in the course of duty. Gloucestershire won by 18 runs. Everyone went home talking of Zaheer's century and Shepherd's tone-up for the next Olympics.

There are not many funny stories about Zaheer himself. He looks studious in those rather severe spectacles and although he smiles often, to reflect a generosity of spirit, he doesn't say amusing things. He's conventional, unexceptional in demeanour, God-fearing; he has no bizarre habits or mannerisms. He chuckles to himself if one of the players comes up with a new joke, or the latest imaginative anecdote about Geoff Boycott or Ian Botham is being gleefully retailed. Zed is never the instigator of the joke or the anecdote.

When he made his first diffident appearance in the West Country, club officials and local sub editors couldn't make up their mind how his name should be spelt—Zahir or Zaheer? He advised the latter. The players, with their aptitude for matey shorthand, preferred Zed. And so it stuck. Every county cricketer in England calls him Zed. The endearing fashion has also been taken up, I've noticed, by some of his Pakistan colleagues.

This is the story of him both as a man and a cricketer. He is sensitive to criticism. He can be deeply hurt. With some insensitivity, the Pakistan cricket board overlooked him when they wanted another captain—not once but several times. It is hard to say whether he has leadership qualities and whether he would have been assertive enough to mould a vastly assorted and, in some cases, temperamental Pakistan Test team. But logically, in terms of record and seniority, he should have been a strong candidate.

Zaheer, we can imagine, passionately wanted to be captain of his country. At least three times he must have been strongly in the running. It has been said that a public statement of his, implying that he longed for the honour, acted against him. I cannot believe that the cricket board, whatever their rather eccentric judgments and methods of operation over the years, would be that petty. A number of the senior players, with whom he had played his Test cricket around the world, privately and publicly advocated his claims. But the call did not come. It must have appeared like a shattering rejection when the young, still immature Javed Miandad was eventually appointed instead.

As we know, Javed did not stay in charge for long. He was the victim of an unprecedented backlash of feeling among most of the other players. The revolt, during and after the cheerless Australian tour of 1981–82, was perhaps the most extraordinary internal wrangle in the history of international cricket. Zaheer was a first-hand witness. His account, later in this book, is detailed and frank. It is none the less absorbing for being so subjective.

A spaced succession of events in Zaheer's career has been hurtful to him. I sense that he was puzzled and disappointed at the way Gloucestershire delayed awarding him his county cap. Some of his early form, as he warily conditioned himself to green seamers' wickets, was tentative. But he argued that he had already scored two double centuries for Pakistan and had acquired an undisputed reputation as a top international batsman by the time his county made their tardy gesture. Privately he was hurt by the way Pakistan crowds with short memories and insensitive souls turned with raucous displeasure at times against their own erstwhile idols like himself. More recently, when on tour with the Pakistan side in the summer of 1982, he became anxious and uneasy about reports, however unsubstantiated they may have appeared to some, that his future with Gloucestershire looked in jeopardy. The county had brought in from Lancashire League cricket a West Indian pace bowler, Franklyn Stephenson, and no-one seemed to be saying how they would apportion the allocation of matches for 'overseas' players in 1983. In addition, Zaheer was worried about his approaching benefit. He had already written to the county, asking for the benefit to be delayed as he had such limited time to organise it.

The county chairman, Don Perry, blamed the press for speculating about Zaheer's future. His loudspeaker announcement during the Cheltenham Festival again rapped our knuckles. But it seemed to be a topic that justified public debate. Zed, holed-up in his various tour hotels and vulnerably remote from committee room machinations in Bristol and Cheltenham, said on one rather poignant occasion to me: 'How I wish I knew what was happening to me.'

Gloucestershire, who with some irony had gone on record as saying, in effect, that they were turning from a policy of incorporating overseas players ('We want an all-English side by the mid 1980s') were now bringing in another West Indian. Bowlers win matches and the capable, likeable Stephenson's arrival made some sense. But at what cost? Sadiq's county career seemed on the point of being sacrificed in any case, because of the overseas registration rule. Now what of Zaheer, one of the world's most stylish batsmen and one, as future generations will see, whose formidable achievements place him forever on the lofty heights of Gloucestershire grandeur?

County officials travelled north, to placate him with news that he was still wanted. Subsequent statements made it clear Zed would be back, at least in 1983, and that his benefit was, of course, going ahead. A few of us with mischievous journalistic imaginations still worried aloud about how the matches would be distributed among the overseas players, batsman and bowler, in 1983.

The controversy aroused surprisingly strong feelings in the boozy bastions of Bristol, where cricket is talked until closing time. Some supporters, bothered by signs of Zaheer's deteriorating health, wondered whether his illustrious career was beginning to tail off. They felt that the county's paramount need was for another penetrative fast bowler to take over from Procter. A search around the English by-ways had been unavailing. So it had to be the West Indian conveyor belt.

Fears 'of a possible abrupt departure by Zaheer conversely prompted what must have been for him a wave of West Country loyalty. One member started a petition and soon had enough signatures to call for a special meeting. It never quite came to that. But the volume of support cheered Zaheer immensely.

He was looking especially vulnerable as I sat with him in his hotel room high above Russell Square in London. The tourists were playing in Leicester and he had been left behind for medical treatment. He had a mouth full of ulcers, a sore throat and an ailing stomach. He was surrounded, almost comically, by pills and other forms of medication. He looked weary and underweight. It was a recurrence of the illness that had struck him in Bristol earlier in the season, when he lost two stone in weight and pleaded with his wife to hurry back to England and provide him with regular meals again.

No-one appeared too certain what was wrong with him. Glandular fever and food poisoning were mentioned. He subscribed to one doctor's diagnosis that it was a form of allergy. 'I think I'm allergic to Chinese food,' he said with childlike acknowledgment of the medico's words. He wasn't quite sure if he would regain his strength in time for the next Test, less than a week away. Somehow he did. I watched him on television, conserving his energies on the field.

Before I left him in his London hotel, he confided that events back in Gloucestershire had taken him by surprise. He had understood that he would be with the county for another four years. His clouded features lit up when we talked about the petition.

I have gone to pains to list some of the events, some minor and even allowed to grow out of proportion, that he has taken as personal blows. They have compounded the hurt to a fragile nature.

I have no doubt at all that they have contributed to a subtle change in the personality of Zaheer. Others have noticed it. Najma, his wife, has noticed it. Those close to him, in the cricketing sense, in both Pakistan and England have noticed it. He has become more wary, more cynical even, more likely to question a proposition put to him. Intikhab, a personal friend of Zed's and a wily psychologist in his own right, told me: 'He's shy and quiet. But he's also now a dogmatic person. If he wants to do something, he must do it. We must appreciate his ways and mannerisms. We must keep him happy.'

Zaheer acknowledges that he has changed gradually in character—and in batting. One of his strengths as a cricketer is that he has always been open to advice. He talks to and, more often, watches other great players. He is prepared at any time to revise his technique. Without tampering with his rich natural basic gifts of batsmanship, he likes to experiment with the more peripheral crafts of the crease. His backlift has lessened. We are now inclined to see him, in the fashion of the day, posed with horizontal bat as the bowler pounds in. If a varying technique doesn't suit him, he immediately reverts to the old style.

He tells us in this book that above all, like all his playing colleagues, he has been fashioned by the land where he was born. Whenever I have seen Pakistan in action, I've been engrossed by the instinctive way that they, like no other cricketing nation, reflect their native prejudices and pride. Their politicians have squabbled and one domestic crisis after another has surfaced during Pakistan's brief history. Prime Minister Bhutto was hanged. So much of the widespread bloodshed has been inexplicable to Western eyes.

From the confused and abrasive early steps, faltering though defiant, Pakistan's cricketers have emerged. They, too, are abrasive. They have a physical and an intellectual swagger. They have something to prove to the world. Their fast bowlers, like Imran, are handsome and flamboyant; they have a slightly arrogant disdain for the conventions. At the Oval in 1954 they won a Test match on their first visit to England. They beat England again at Lord's in 1982. These were triumphant gestures of soaring stature. At home, free sweets were distributed, horns blared and streets were thronged.

No national cricket side is more excitable. It manifests itself in scenes that irritate alien spectators. The players, quick-tempered and thin-skinned, are pained and puzzled on occasions when they find they have made the headlines yet again. But they are combative by nature. Many of them, not least the exquisite stroke-makers and the beguiling leg-spinners have rich and rare talents.

Pakistan was only admitted to the Imperial Cricket Conference in 1952. From the days of Abdul Hafeez Kardar, policeman Fazal Mahmood and the pacy Khan Mohammad, whom I had watched once or twice playing for Somerset in the early fifties—the three of them helped to beat England in 1954, when the home selectors had aberrations and Hutton mishandled badly as captain—right through an accomplished line to Hanif Mohammad, Mushtaq Mohommad, Intikhab Alam, Asif Iqbal and Majid Khan, up to Imran's teams, bountiful individual skills have been paraded. At times I have thrilled to the rhythmic stroke play and picturesque spin bowling, anomalously summoned up, and considered Pakistan so nearly the best in the world. It is an achievement of great merit. Yet I remember what Trevor Bailey wrote in *A History of Cricket*. He warmly praised Pakistan's strides forward and then went on to say: 'The one big criticism of Pakistan cricket is that it has probably been run too rigidly. Although this discipline has its good points, it has inevitably been responsible for several clashes between the authorities and the players, especially those who have become accustomed to the easier and financially more rewarding life of a top class cricketer in England. Some of their managers appeared to be under the impression that they were leading a platoon rather than a group of cricketers from very different backgrounds. This would not have mattered if they had possessed a greater knowledge of the game or the psychology of cricketers . . .'

There was no doubt an indignant reaction to such home-truths. Many of the players knew how perceptive and accurate Mr Bailey's assessment was.

During the tentative transition from matting to turf, Pakistan seemed at times to be losing its way. We read of the slow scoring, the flat wickets, the obsession about avoiding defeat. Tactics could be inexplicable and sometimes an unsubtle yawn. Pakistan let the initiative slip away by what appeared, at least to outsiders, to be a negative, ultra-cautious approach. Where did they go wrong at Edgbaston in 1971 when Zed had been so magnificent? Or at Leeds the same summer? It was often difficult to accept the rationale. Why did stroke-makers choose to withdraw into somnolent recesses? Why did the capable Mudassar determine his place in the record books with the cussedly slowest Test century on record at Lahore? It dragged on for 557 minutes.

Pakistan cricket has always mystified and intrigued me as much as it has fascinated me. Someone worked out that there had been 14 captains in one period of less than 30 years. I gave up counting long before and only sympathised with most of those, some with negligible leadership aptitude, who did their best for the few nominal matches they were in control.

Again to the outsider, it was never easy to sort out where governmental intrusion ended and cricket began. The politics frequently obscured the wickets.

'Keep in with the Board' was canny advice for ambitious players. Zaheer, I would suggest, wasn't good at this. He didn't mix socially with the Board members. If there was a masonic layer, he was usually outside it.

For years, players seemed to be in and out of favour. Intikhab was a respected skipper and was liked by the English team. He had an intimate working knowledge of English conditions and must have given the Board immeasurable pleasure by leading his country through an England tour without a single defeat. But he, too, had the captaincy taken from him. He wasn't even in the squad for the 1975 World Cup.

He has a comfortable build and an accessible, sophisticated manner. He knows cricket's tricks of the trade and the armament of psychological warfare between bat, pad and silly mid-off. No cricket sweater wool is easily pulled over his eyes. He can be tough—and gentle.

I talked at some length with him about man management during the 1982 tour. 'It is vital for the captain and manager to get to know the boys well. I accepted the job of manager because they wanted someone who had played the game and was currently involved in cricket. I have been very happy with the response. From the outset I talked to the boys individually and collectively. Most of the trouble on tours comes from a communications gap.'

I tried in vain to prod Intikhab into a considered comment on the nagging problems that involved Javed Miandad and the senior players. He was too diplomatic. 'I wasn't involved personally. It was very unfortunate, I agree. But I must say it was a very kind gesture on Javed's part to step down from the captaincy. I don't accept that this was a case of player-power, as everyone appears to think. Again it was this sad lack of communication. There was no-one around to sort it out at the time. You can only do that if you are close to the players.

'It takes a long time to get to know 16 or 17 of them. But if you have the necessary personality and an inside knowledge of the game, you should quickly gain their respect. Remember, there are 16 or 17 different minds. Your job is to get to know and understand each one. To know what each individual is like. How he plays. How he dresses. What he likes to eat. He may have a financial problem—or a domestic one. The manager's job is to get to know their hearts. When they are happy, he is happy.'

As a piece of fundamental psychology, it seemed flawless to me. I would unreservedly recommend it to managing directors, trade union leaders and sporting bosses.

* * *

Zaheer's batting has at times bordered on genius. Cricket writers have sighed in wonderment at his artistry and implied, in their spontaneous prose, that in such innings he has no peer.

There is none of the whiplash venom and magnificent muscle that you get from Richards or Botham. They are inclined to use a bat as an instrument of battle. Zed uses it as an instrument of music. He caresses the handle on the way to the wicket as if it were a violin. He believes it incapable of an ugly note. In one-day cricket, he will occasionally copy one of the game's artful improvisers and the ball will loop in unworthy fashion to alien territory in the outfield. His admirers keep their sheepish silence; they can imagine well enough his self-reproach. You see him later and he knows what you are thinking. 'I had to slog,' he says, as if asking for forgiveness.

Like no-one perhaps since Bradman, he is obsessed with making runs. In a month of full flow, records tumble in quick succession and he's called a run-machine, just as Bradman was. Yet in truth, they have few similarities. Their style, their build, their mentality are different. What they have had in common is an utterly insatiable appetite for scoring runs.

As Najma his wife will confirm with laughter in her lovely eyes, Zed makes centuries every night in his sleep. He wakes thinking of centuries. He relishes his scoring shots with a disproportionate joy. His philosophy of life is geared not simply to his cricket but to being at the wicket. He has a minimal interest in many of the mundane aspects of our daily life. He

22

doesn't even enjoy fielding. He embraces batting with an unmitigated passion.

Whenever I ask him to recall his best innings, he replies without hesitation: 'All those when I had big scores.'

Nothing better sums up Zaheer Abbas as he poises those slender shoulders for a century of centuries. . . . and then on to the next target.

Records have the magnetic appeal of a drug. There is no simpering, affected modesty when he tells you that he wants to go on scoring centuries. 'A low score means nothing in the record book.' He doesn't recoil from the notion that he's playing for posterity. 'If you dont as a batsman, make really big scores, what's the point?'

Some county cricketers profess not to know or care about their statistics. Zaheer is unfailingly motivated by the knowledge of his. He'll wander into the scorebox at the county ground in Bristol to talk to scorer, Bert Avery, a good friend and confidant. 'How many more do I need to reach Wally Hammond's number of centuries?' he asks with a winsome optimism.

'You won't get that far, Zed,' says Bert, with a fleeting glance up from the copper-plate writing that is famed on the circuit.

Hammond, with 113 hundreds for Gloucestershire, is well out of Zaheer's reach. Not so, the batsman mentally decides, Tom Graveney, W. G. Grace, Arthur Milton and Alf Dipper, the yeoman opener from Tewkesbury. No-one seems too sure how much longer Zaheer will be around in the West Country but he would clearly like to crack one or two records before he goes home for good.

Bert is custodian of Zed's expensive wristwatch as well as his records. After the almost flawless 216 and 156—without being dismissed—at the Oval in 1976, Zaheer was thrilled to receive from the scorer a beautifully produced chart, showing the direction of every single scoring shot. It was a work of great detail and accuracy, and a copy was taken home with great pride to his father. Zed never failed to return without a little present for Bert and eventually, with some irony, a wristwatch.

It was from Bert Avery I heard the story, confirmed by

Grahame Parker, the former secretary-manager and other members of the county side, of the Sunday fixture at Arundel in 1972. The incident is one of those that is retold with affection and chortles at the distance of a decade. One or two senior officials were somewhat twitchy at the time. Gloucestershire were playing at Edgbaston on the Saturday and they had to journey down to Sussex on the Sunday morning. Newcomer Zaheer relied implicitly on Sadiq who, for his part, according to colleagues, used Northampton and Mushtaq's connections as the beloved compass point for virtually every cross-country commitment. 'Arundi? Ver is that?' asked the good-natured Sadiq, who is said by Alastair Hignell still to get his vs and ws mixed up. 'Don't vorry. Ve'll find it.'

They did—at an embarrassingly late hour. The car, radiator boiling, chugged into the delightful Arundel ground at just about the time the players were due on the field. Procter, who was standing in for Tony Brown as captain, had already handed in a team-list while fearful of its ultimate composition. At least he was able to field first and two substitutes were tactfully dredged up. Zaheer changed faster than ever before. Club brimstone was directed on the unlucky Sadiq as the car driver. He was left out. 'But ve vere given vrong instructions,' he protested.

Everything ended well. Zaheer was invited to send down six overs—maybe as part punishment—and gave away only 31 runs. Arthur Milton made one of his intermittent appearances as a languid medium-pacer to take two prized wickets. Procter bowled beautifully (5–10), David Shepherd beefed beautifully (68 not out) and Gloucestershire won by two wickets.

It is true to say that the unlikely front-seat combination of Zed and Sad would never win a car rally, despite so many unscheduled practice runs.

But I must revert to the theme of batting triumphs. Let us start with his double centuries for his county. I missed scarcely a ball in that 1977 match at Cheltenham when, against Sussex, he scored 205 and 108. He'd become the first batsman in the world to make a double and single century in the same match three times. The previous season he had done it against Kent at Canterbury and Surrey at the Oval. Not once was he dismissed. Zaheer has always, with commendable honesty, made the point that he is either very good indeed—or very bad. Others have noted this strange, disconcerting pattern in his career. There have been whole series as a Test player when he has looked weighed down by the sheer complexity of his task. The bat has not belonged to the batsman.

I have heard his devotees talk of a schizophrenic element in his batting. That has invariably appeared to me too dramatic an interpretation of his flights of form. He's not physically strong and I believe he is not equipped to play for twelve months of the year. His obsessive wish to inhabit the crease isn't lessened but his zest for stroke-making is. By his own rhythmic and instinctive standards, the reflexes become sluggish and the movement laboured. The eyes show an uncharacteristic weariness. Najma says: 'Then he gets terribly depressed. When he fails at the wicket he isn't easy to console.'

He never once looked like failing during his imperious residence at the crease at Cheltenham in 1977. Sussex's arc of off-side fielders despaired. I can still vividly see them exchanging helpless glances. There was almost a predestined glory about those two innings, as if, with supreme confidence, he was unwrapping them for the record books.

Cheltenham, with its Victorian academic stonework and still perceptible remnants of decorum from a past generation, is made for style. Zaheer was the natural animation for this cherished sporting print as July emerged into August and wisps of cloud scudded playfully from Malvern country to the protective Cotswolds. No-one could have better adorned that picture. It had grace, nobility and monumental class. It belonged to the Golden Age.

As if to reprimand Gloucestershire for pondering so long over his early figures with them and delaying the award of a county cap, he dominated our domestic cricket throughout 1976. Whenever I found myself watching the county he was at the wicket. It was the summer of the drought and he was able to shed his sweaters. He should have been exhausted in the

25

evenings but invariably he was smiling.

'Do you know,' he used to tell me as he unbuckled his pads, 'I aim for 50 . . . and then 100 . . . and then 150 . . . and then 200.' The uncomplicated face of cricketing greatness.

Home in Pakistan there had been early records like the sixth-wicket stand of 353 with Salah-ud-Din for Karachi against what was then East Pakistan in 1968–9. Salah-ud-Din scored 256 and the young Zaheer was cross with himself when he was out for . . . 197.

By 1981 I was frantically permutating the passages of purple prose. I'd long since exhausted my supply of eulogistic adjectives. Yet it had rained most of May and I accompanied him as he paced the pavilion and outfields in unbridled impatience. He didn't face a ball in a county match until early June. 'Oh dear, I must make up for that,' he said.

And so he did: in a wondrous way that was often poetic and never prosaic. He scored 1,000 runs in 27 days of June. Only Len Hutton (1949) and Mike Smith (1959) had reached this aggregate in a single month since the war. W. G. Grace and Hammond had previously managed it for Gloucestershire.

I shall certainly miss other statistical peaks in Zaheer's batting. Forgive me, Zed. They interest me less than the spirit, style and elegance with which the runs are made.

But it would be wrong and reprehensible of me to overlook the Gloucester Festival of 1982 when, as I remember writing in *The Guardian*, the thunderclouds kept changing ends and storming in over long-on in the late afternoon every day. The gatemen were cheery as ever there but the crowds were poor and everyone was wondering how much longer the local council would help to fund a cricket week based on warm memories— and distinctive, triumphant LBW appeals from Tom Goddard, who lived down the road—rather than current enthusiasm.

As it happened, the apathy was almost criminal. Far too many people missed Zaheer's century in each innings against Lancashire. It was the seventh time he had done it, and it put him level with Wally Hammond in the world records. He had systematically, prodded by Bert Avery's kindly words in the ear, overtaken the likes of Bradman, Graveney, Jessop, Hendren and Sutcliffe (four times), C. B. Fry (five times) and Jack Hobbs (six). He had no intention of sharing the title with Hammond for too long; in just over six months, at Karachi, the record was his alone.

During those two Gloucester innings, Zaheer was a sick man. I'm still none too sure how he summoned up the reserves of energy. His wife had stayed behind in Pakistan for a family wedding and Zaheer was making a bad job of feeding himself. He phoned her and she detected how lonely and ill he was. Between his innings he told me: 'Najma will be back in Bristol tomorrow.' The thought of having his wife and adored daughters back at his side before long seemed to inspire him.

I have gone to many players, ex-players and officials in an attempt to evaluate an international cricketer of such stature. Some see him as phlegmatic, moody, inconsistent and even self-centred. None of them speak ill of him as a batsman. None of them say a solitary word in disparagement of his exceptional, largely uncoached, skills.

At Worcester in mid-afternoon, against the mellifluous background of the cathedral bells, I talked to his Tourist colleagues. They looked on him as something of an elder statesman, slightly elevated and distant, a quiet, respected figure.

They had no doubts about his place in the history of Pakistan cricket. 'We watch him and copy him,' said one. 'His weakness is the extremes of form,' said another. 'He's a gentleman ...' 'A deep one, oh yes, a deep one ...'

Later in this match, during which he happened to score the 94th century of his career, I exluded everything else—even the Cathedral bells and the plum orchard accents all round me on the lovely ground—and concentrated on Zaheer. He strolled around the outfield, returning the ball with precise judgment to the wicket keeper but seeming to hope that not too many shots would be aimed in his direction. At the wicket he was neat and absolutely unemotional. He was so different from some of the others. Stray thoughts chased back and made me chuckle: of Imran's demonstrative contretemps with Mike Brearley at

Lord's in 1980, of Sarfrez's unplayable deliveries that had a pained Bedi conceding the one-day match in 1978, of Sikander kicking down the stumps, and Asif threatening to call off the rest of the tour against India, of the unpredictable flamboyance of Javed. And here was Zed, so apparently placid and imperturbable. Yet I knew from what he had told me that slights could be harboured and displeasure could simmer.

I asked Intikhab what he made of him. 'You don't need me to tell you. He's one of our very best—lovely to watch. It's so difficult to know where to bowl to him. Runs just flow from his bat. I have no doubt which was his finest knock—the one on the rain-affected wicket against Kent at Gravesend in 1971. The ball was turning and popping. And, as we all knew, Underwood had to be the best in the world in those conditions. Zaheer made a fantastic 100. He made so many unbelievable shots on that, his first tour.'

I asked Gloucestershire's current captain David Graveney. 'Zed is one of the finest players of left-arm spin, as Derek Underwood will confirm. He's the most clinical dispatcher of a bad ball I've ever seen. He never misses an opportunity and it always gets through the field. When he came first he had the kind of backlift that was particularly suitable on overseas wickets where the ball didn't do so much off the pitch. His best shot has to be off the back foot through the off-side. Zed's never stood still. He's open to new ideas and in his quiet way is helpful to the young county batsmen—he never forces his views or advice on them.'

But what about the appearance he occasionally gives of being just a little less than enthusiastic about taking the field? 'Playing for nearly 12 months of the year, it must become difficult to motivate himself every single day.'

In terms of sheer, grinding practice and application, Graveney nominates Zaheer as 'the model professional.' The Gloucestershire skipper is a canny observer of the human condition and he has seen Zaheer, over ten years or so, in ecstatic and dejected moods, even though that sweeping range of emotions is manifested with the minimum of flourish.

'It's seemed to me that his greatest excitement is shown when he takes a wicket. I won't forget his first for us. The victim was Farokh Engineer. For all kinds of nationalistic reasons he didn't see the joke. Zed and Sadiq thought it was highly amusing!' For another Bristol-based assessment I turned to David Green. He has now reached the press box by way of the first class game and the catering industry. He's a talkative, supposedly cynical and likeable companion. His language is salty. He'll talk of cricket or modern poetry with equal passion and sensitivity. His judgment is considered and usually spot-on. This is what he says about Zaheer:

'He's as handsome a stroke-maker as I have ever seen. The beauty and elegance of his off-side play is such that it's not difficult to imagine his gracing cricket's Golden Age ...' (we can't get away from it, can we) ... 'Zaheer is not blessed with the physique of a Dexter or a Vivian Richards, so his desire to hit the ball far and often is necessarily met by methods different from theirs. The Edwardian grace of the batting is not merely show, a flourish added to please the eye of the spectator. The strokes are wristy. The follow-through is high and free because by such means, maximum force is applied to the ball with the minimum expenditure of pure strength. And always beneath the surface there's a technique as solid as rock. He's sometimes caught at slip and gulley in a way that, say, Boycott would not be. But Zed is a man unwilling to watch passively as bowlers direct the ball wide of his stumps. He wishes to dominate, and backs his eye and skill where lesser players opt for inactivity.'

That is an inside and academic viewpoint; it's also a shrewd, human one. The blond, buoyant Green, and eminently breezy opening bat once with Lancashire and Gloucestershire, also chased balls outside the off-stump. He was more fallible than Zaheer: it was part of his persona.

Keith Ball, a cricket historian and statistician who has watched Zaheer many times over ten years or so, sees him as 'an artist with an artist's eye for the game ... He tries to make every stroke a thing of beauty in itself.'

In the course of a charming little essay on Zaheer, he writes: 'His cricketing career is based on a desire to be remembered as one of the outstanding batsmen of his era. Unlike some others with the same lofty ideals, Zaheer could never be described as selfish. A spectator, after watching him play a long innings, could not leave the ground feeling that Zaheer was playing for himself.

'At the wicket he has the same grandeur as Archie MacLaren—the extraordinary backlift and full swing of the bat, powerful forward strokes combined with strong back-foot play. His stance is relaxed but watchful, a panther ready to spring. He is not a "killer" like Viv Richards or Don Bradman. His strokes do not insult the bowler . . . He is a cricketer who adds aesthetic values and delight to lovers of the game who are not interested in percentages and hours at the crease.

'In Zaheer's batting, beauty and orthodoxy are perfectly harmonised. Lithe, strong of wrist, quick in eye and foot, he has no cause or inclination to fear any bowler. In his style, the perfection of poise and grace are enshrined for ever . . .'

We have heard Intikhab's unqualified vote for Zed's best innings. The Pakistan captain for that 1971 match at Gravesend must have been influenced by the sheer spunk and apparent maturity from one so new to Test cricket.

There were, of course, the centuries before lunch, lively and tuneful as the morning lark: at Worcester, Northampton, Bath and, in 1978, at Bristol where the New Zealanders suffered recurrent optical illusions in the deep off-side field.

We could pluck any of half a dozen majestic parades of his artistry during his golden harvest of runs in 1976. Tony Lewis put them all together in *The Cricketer* and wrote: 'When he walks to the wicket he looks too lean to hit the ball far. His spectacles suggest a certain vulnerability. His cheeks are narrow and hollow, and his bundle of sweaters tells how he feels the cold . . . His cover driving is dazzling . . . His great art is to hit the fairly straight ball which is well up to him through cover. I suppose he plays slightly inside the line. Whatever the method, he is almost impossible to restrain in this form.'

My eyes shined idolatrously, well outside the line of objective journalistic duty, as he again earned the unofficial Freedom of Cheltenham. His average there alone was well over 200 and when he moved on to Southampton, he scored another perfunctory century to give him an extraordinary 413 from three innings—without being dismissed.

It was at Cheltenham that I heard a perspiring and exasperated Sussex outfielder wail to no-one in particular as he retrieved yet another rebound off the rails: 'We won't get this bloody bloke out if we wait till Cheltenham next year!' It was all the more earthy, hearing it as I did immediately after the discreet, well-rounded vowels of my canvas retreat where for the whole week of the Festival the single most aggressive act is the crunch of teaspoon on sugar.

Zaheer is himself always tempted to cite his maiden Test in England. The double century at Birmingham was a sweet segment from sport's romantic fiction. He would never again make such impact, would never again be the overnight hero of every schoolboy and student in his homeland.

Those who regularly chronicle the fortunes of the Pakistan team might more likely turn to the country's home series with India in 1978. The two were playing against each other again after 18 years. Zaheer was supreme and Pakistan won the series. His average from the three Tests was 194.33. Without swagger or the demeanour of a star, he captivated the spectators on every ground and looked the best, certainly the most elegant, batsman in the world.

The Packer Boys were back again, being embraced and wanting to make a few personal points to supersede the surfeit of hypocrisy. At Faisalabad, a new Test venue, he scored 176. Hussain Syed reported in *The Cricketer*: 'Zaheer was at his brilliant best. His off-driving could not have been surpassed and anything short was punished severely. I have seen him play some fine innings all over the world but this was certainly his greatest. The fourth wicket partnership with Miandad of 255 was a record for Pakistan against India.'

That was the first Test. Some said his 235 not out at Lahore in the second Test was even more memorable. The atmosphere was heady. It was Pakistan's first win over India for 26 years. Yes, of course, there was a national holiday. I'm reminded that Zed ended the match with a six. Who said he lacked a theatrical sense?

Rudaba and Roshana, his adored daughters who bring him luck—
and Najma and Zed so much joy.

When he first played for Gloucestershire I wrote that he reminded me of a choirboy. There was that starched, well-laundered look. As a cricketer he's impeccably turned-out. He has a fetish almost about his shirts and collars being properly ironed. Najma told me: 'When we were married first I didn't know how to iron shirts. Zaheer taught me! He was very particular.'

He bats with his shirt sleeves buttoned at the wrist. Everything about him is tidy—and slightly fragile. His face is intense; he thinks and he calculates all the time he's at the wicket. He doesn't arouse antagonisms. Close fielders and belligerent bowlers don't bother him with tricks of intimidation; they wouldn't have too much effect, and they know it. I motor home from a game, savouring again just one drive off the back foot wide of extra cover—or the image of him going up on his toes, like no other player in the present game, to square-cut.

At times his introspection must trouble his team-mates. He can look moody—and he can look positively indolent in the field. But never once has he been less than courteous to me. We've chatted on players' balconies, in Bristol pubs (where we share 'tonics'), hotel lounges and, during one tour game in 1982, on opposite sides of the boundary ropes.

I can detect the influence of parental discipline, a Moslem faith and a well-ordered family life. If Zed is vague, uncomplicated and impractical, his wife redresses the balance. His daughters, he says, bring him luck. When he returns home, to devote more time to the family construction business, he will leave us in England with his most cherished possession—his records.

He'll be generously and timelessly represented in a county already rich with the silken talents of Grace and Jessop, Hammond and Graveney.

*   *   *

With felicitous timing—helped by old fashioned journalistic instinct—I flew into Lahore on the day in December 1982 that

33

Zaheer scored his 100th century. That cunning old pocket calculator of a batsman had stage-managed it for a Test match. I knew he would do it; the adrenalin was racing, Lahore was a lucky ground for him and he was mentally attuned for the achievement. As almost an after-thought he went on to a splendid 215.

My auto rickshaw driver was doubtless caught up in the heady excitement of the occasion. The ride was even more precariously exhilarating than usual. My driver splashed through the pools of water that still lay on the side of the road outside the Gaddafi Stadium. In one movement he pocketed his rupees and pointed me in the direction of the nearest entrance. Vendors of Cola and curried snacks all round the circular ground were not short of customers. The cricket, I quickly discovered to my bewilderment, was being less generously patronised.

Could this be Lahore, I naively asked myself? I had read of the bulging crowds when the Indians were last there in 1978. Now they were back in the first Test of a six-match series—and there seemed to be more police than spectators to watch the play. At times during Zaheer's marvellous history-making innings the attendance was no more than two to three thousand. Intikhab threw his arms into the air and there was considerable sadness in his voice. 'There should have been 50 or even 60 thousand to cheer that feat of Zed's. It was quite fantastic.' And so said the Indian captain, Sunil Gavaskar with whom I was to spend some time in the next few days.

I saw the Pakistan players gazing disbelievingly through the windows of the dressing room. You felt they were embarrassed for their illustrious team-mate as he paraded his wristy and classical repertoire.

There were immediate post mortems, of course. Everyone appeared to be in agreement that cricket was suddenly costing too much. Mr Mian Azizul Haq Qureshi, an entrepreneur from Sargodha, had caused a stir by buying-out the whole series on behalf of Paasban Finance Corporation. The BCCP had sold the rights—including the one day matches—for one crore and 62 lakhs rupees, (about £810,000) the kind of figure that was probably hard to resist. But under the new set-up, enclosure tickets for the five days of a Test were being raised from 400–500 rupees to 1,500 (just under £100 at the exchange rate of the time). The result was that Friday, a holiday, attracted a pathetically small crowd. There was widespread comment in the newspapers, on radio and television. It was ironic that several thousand potential cricket supporters, in the northern Indian city of Amristar had been trying over zealously and in vain—and withstanding some beefy policy baton charges—to obtain visas to attend the match in Pakistan.

Admission prices eventually came down and crowds improved. But as that engaging bank clerk and spin bowler Iqbal Qasim said: 'The momentum of the match had gone by then.' I was sorry Iqbal wasn't playing but Pakistan had gone for pace.

Sarfraz was back at the last minute—and bowling beautifully. The buzz in the lofty press box was that he was going for good after this match. He had said so much in that extravagant style of his. But he took four cheap wickets and talk of retirement was conveniently shelved.

Zed was again a national hero, whatever the size of the crowd. He was feted at one private party after another in Lahore. He sent for his wife and children to join him. My wife and I were also kindly taken along as his personal guests. At one party the television set was wheeled in and we watched a re-run of the shot that brought Zaheer his 100th hundred. He chuckled as he saw how he lofted his bat horizontally above his head. 'Just like Geoff Boycott did when he got his 100th,' said Zed, revealing an impressionable side to his nature.

The parties, in the way of sophisticated Lahore, were hospitable, yet strangely formal to a western guest. The men and the women, uniformly beautiful it seemed to me, were segregated. The conversation was pleasantly muted. At one party we sat on cushions in the bedroom; alas, it has been chosen for its size rather than innuendo. We sat cross-kneed, praising the principal guest out of earshot (it seemed inappropriate to bestow our congratulations with verbal vigour) and exchanging philosophical pearls on ertswhile colonialism.

35

Gavaskar and Doshi came at Zaheer's invitation to some of the parties. 'All Indians are my friends,' he confided to me. Another guest was the Pakistan singer and film star Nadeen, whose prolific output of pictures is only matched by his hauls of wickets in former days as an off-spinner. 'We are old friends,' Zaheer told me. 'He went to Islamia College like me—and we both played for Park Crescent.' The latter statement was made with the smiling confirmation of true friendship. Club cricket at that level carried an especial bond.

Back at the ground the bad weather returned. Most of the Pakistan players listened with cosmopolitan zeal to rock music on the swish cassette player. Zaheer chatted to me and then retired to snooze in the 'Doctor's Consultation Office.' The delightful Iqbal, armed with a mountain of autograph books, gave me misgivings about the banking profession as he demonstrated a deft versatility of signature. And to think I had only previously seen those magical fingers wrapped beguilingly round the ball.

In Lahore I day-dreamed about Zaheer's magnificent double century as, with my wife, I explored the mosques, mausoleums and monuments. We strolled across the Gymknana where, on half a dozen matting wickets, fragile schoolboys fantasized that one day they would bowl like Imran. Many of the present Test team had probably done just that, on this same expanse of khaki-green turf a few years earlier.

Back in my hotel room I discovered that Zaheer was rightly on the front page of The *Pakistan Times*. I felt elated for him and yet wished there had not been so many grey-jerseyed police sitting around grim-faced at the Gaddafi Stadium and that one had not put an aggressively restraining arm on my shoulder as I attempted to take some innocuous family film on my unsophisticated cine camera outside the ground.

The President, Mohammad Zia-ul-Haq, name suitably abbreviated, was featured in almost every headline and most of the pictures. He was currently engaged on a delicate visit to America, where he was having talks with President Reagan and having to pronounce on the military present in Afghanastan, a peaceful atomic energy programme and free elections ('I foresee

36

them in about two years' time'). From his reply to an American journalist I also learned something of his philosophy towards flogging. 'Under the Islamic law we have introduced flogging. It is a punishment to be given not as a matter of degradation of man but as a deterrent—something in which man is made to repent. Flogging is done in a style where a man repents, yet is not humiliated.'

Transgressors who drink, gamble or sexually philander are vulnerable to a lashing in Pakistan. There was one in Lahore while I was there. I shuddered when I heard about it next day. But this is a book about Pakistan cricket, not Pakistan politics. It is not my business to analyse the coup of 1978 or ponder whether the cosmetic signs of democracy against an unlikely backcloth of rigid Islamic principles is what the people want.

I returned again to the Stadium, where the animated chatter of Punjabi had increased and the ladies' enclosure, deserted in the early days of the first Test, was again filling up with red-lipped beauties in their iridescent dresses. The sun was shining once more. Someone wanted Zed to bask still in the glory of his double hundred. 'It was such a dull day,' the batsman said, teeth-fleshing, the memory filling him again with sunlight.

In truth he was on his way to his fifth century in a row, two of them in one-day matches. He was batting as well as I'd ever seen: dainty, perfectly balanced, ruthless with the bad ball. The ball streaked to the boundary not by muscle but by perfection of timing. He made so much of current cricket look shoddy.

When I left Delhi, bound for Lahore, the Indian nation still seemed in a state of shock over the humiliating way Pakistan had beaten them 7–1 in the Asian Games hockey final. Re-criminations were loud and unsparing. I mused on the possibility of a vengeful approach by Gavaskar's players. In fact, as the Test match went into its early days, an almost second string India beat Pakistan, the Esanda World Hockey Tournament favourites, 2–1 at Melbourne. Revenge was sweet and the *Pakistan Times* hockey correspondent, Farooq Mazhar, mystified by such an illogical reversal, began his lament: 'Hells bells!'

Zed had never been a hockey player ('It always appeared a bit

37

too rough'). His mind at Lahore was on more personal matters. 'Let me see, I think I need another 50 or so to complete my 1,000 runs against India. And, what is it, three hundred and something for 4,000 Test runs ...?' There was never a better form of motivation. The younger brother, home in Karachi, was coming up with all the latest figures.

Success at Lahore carried a suitably tangible recompense. Wills announced a sizeable cash bonus for Zaheer, and so did his friends back in Sailkot, where he was born. Other perks followed. It would be wrong to suggest that cash comforts like this didn't delight him, although I never found him obsessively mercenary in the way of so many professional sportsmen.

He went on making centuries in that series against what often looked like a demoralised India side. The sight of Zaheer commanding the crease would have demoralised any team. Future generations, not just in Pakistan, will talk of his treasured talents and pretend that they were present.

In the following pages, he tells with refreshing candour his story: of fulfillment and frustration, of his undeviating preoccupation for scoring runs, of challenges on and off the pitch.

DAVID FOOT

POLITICS

My Unhappiest Tour

Everyone seems to think that Pakistan cricket is bedevilled by political intrigue and whims.

I accept that our relatively brief history is coloured by controversy, much of it bewildering to outsiders' eyes. Our squabbles have become public property and often differences that we would have preferred to keep within our own committee rooms have decorated the world's headlines.

As a young nation we have found ourselves coping with problems never remotely experienced by the old-established cricketing countries. We wear the scars from the horrendous bloodshed that our parents went through. Old national grievances have not all disappeared. Our characteristics of temperament have at times made us impetuous and impassioned.

At the time of Packer, when players of all nations came together to improve their standard of living in defiance of the game's governing bodies, the Pakistan contingent was able to put straight a few misapprehensions. We integrated easily and were not moody, even if our lifestyle was rather more abstemious. We were not obsessed with drawing matches and avoiding defeat at all cost. We relished going for our shots—as surely we demonstrated at times in the 1982 Test series in England.

I am amazed at other misapprehensions about us. Overseas commentators are repeatedly implying that there is a deep, emotional rift between Lahore and Karachi. That is absolute nonsense. There is no real evidence of it. Just look at the composition of our Test side; for the most part we get on well together. In one of the serious English newspapers during 1982 there was an article which said: 'It is a question of Lahore versus Karachi. Apparently some men from the different cities are not even talking to each other ... Imran, although from Karachi, was the only possible captain acceptable to the Lahore-ites for this tour ...' It simply wasn't true.

But it is my duty to be as honest as I can. To foreign eyes, some of the things, contentious and capricious, that have gone on in the so-called interest of Pakistan cricket, have been matters of both fun and folly. We don't enjoy either label. Some of the differences between our Cricket Board and the Test players have been inexplicable to sports lovers from other countries. The varying attitudes have often been inexplicable to us. I am convinced that the relationship has improved immensely. I did badly with the bat during the England Tests in 1982 but the tour party was at all times a happy one. Intikhab Alam, as the manager, and Imran Khan, as the dynamic captain, were jointly responsible for that spirit of cordiality.

A recurrent criticism of the Pakistan players concerns *player-power*. It has an ominous and militant ring to it. The implication is that, in the quaint words of some of my English friends, the tail is wagging the dog. This alleged imbalance isn't confined to cricket, of course. I have read of what is happening more and more in soccer. You are always going to get suspicions of this kind of situation when superstars are in a position to name their own price. That is the way of business: the top product is priceless. I see nothing wrong with this—when the superstar, an Ian Botham or a Kevin Keegan, is able to pull in the crowds on his own.

The world's great sportsmen have become mercenaries. They are doing nothing wrong; they are simply exploiting their considerable personal talents. The only danger is if in the process they disrupt wage structures and dressing rooms, and that rarely happens. During my matches with Gloucestershire, I have heard Somerset cited as a county side in which the players have too much say and muscle. For a start they have three great match-winners in Botham, Viv Richards and Joel Garner. I don't pretend to know whether players like this at Taunton have too much power. What I do know is that they are exceptional match-winners and the spectators come specifically to watch them.

But I stray from player-power allegedly within the Pakistan team. Our critics like to quote chapter and verse. They talk of the protest we staged over poor pay—and I shall come to that later. Fresher in their minds is what took place in Australia in early 1982 and the unrelenting stand taken by the senior players. Javed Miandad, the young, inexperienced captain, was at the centre of this whole, undignified controversy. And so, reluctantly was I.

It led to unprecedented anger and divisions between a captain and his senior players. There were strong words and unfortunate acrimony. The consequences were painful. No-one enjoyed being embroiled in yet another public row. Things were said—and regretted. I feel personally that a great deal, the height of tactlessness, should never have been said in the first place.

I intend to chart the whole sorry incident not to dredge up old ills and to apportion blame. But I feel, in fairness to myself, the record should be put right.

Occasionally I have heard it said that my differences with Javed sprang from jealousy, that I resented the fact this young man had been nominated above me as captain. His appointment was indeed a surprise to me and to many of the other senior players.

In his book, *The Cricket Revolution* Bob Willis writes: 'Apart from Sarfraz and Sadiq, Zaheer is the only one of the elite Pakistanis not to have captained his country, an honour that seems to get passed round a lot. I wonder if that troubles him?'

It is a fair point. Yes, of course, I should have loved to be honoured with the captaincy, a distant dream from the first day I played for Pakistan. It is not a matter of conceit or self-importance. But captaincy of one's country has to be the supreme honour. Friends in the team used to say I was a strong candidate. Compliments from the higher echelons were frequently paid me after a notable innings. My double centuries had made me something of a national idol.

My personality was hardly outgoing but international cricket has been full of introvert skippers who led by example. I liked to think I had some charm and warmth towards my fellow players. I got on well with them without exception. My record as captain for PIA was good and I had led them to tournament successes. I welcomed the added responsibility of being a leader and having a hand, tactically, in the destiny of a match. No Pakistan player ever got more immersed in the game. My wife used to confide to friends: 'Zed loves to lead. He's so involved and I know that he can be a successful and lucky captain for Pakistan.' She also observed that I was profoundly disappointed when I was again overlooked.

As Bob Willis noted, the captaincy has had little permanency in Pakistan cricket over the more recent years.

In just over ten years Pakistan have been led by Intikhab (twice), Majid Khan, Asif Iqbal, Mushtaz Mohammad, Wasim Bari, Javed Miandad and Imran Khan. I don't think I have forgotten anyone!

It isn't the best way to foster a sense of continuity, although the Board would argue that they have always striven, under more than their share of difficulties—with Packer in the middle—to find the best man for the job.

People used to come up to me and say: 'Whatever is the policy? Whenever we lose a Test match, the captain seems to have gone the next day!'

That was an exaggeration, of course. But the captaincy changed with bewildering regularity. My wife once joked: 'They appear to change captains as often as a woman changes a dress.'

It isn't my business to examine why I was never selected as captain of Pakistan. Others decided, I suppose, that I lacked the necessary qualities.

In his introduction to this book, cricket writer David Foot wonders whether I may have prejudiced my chances by not mixing more with members of my Board. It was simply not my style. Others were better at it than I was because that sort of integration did not come naturally to me. Never once in my life have I been a sycophant. I asked only that the Board would judge me as a man—and as a batsman at the wicket.

Because the conflict in Australia concerned Javed and myself I should quickly point out my admiration for him as cricketer. He scored 163 in his first Test against New Zealand at Lahore in 1976–77 and 206 in the same series at his birthplace, Karachi. He has a fine technique and should have many runs ahead of him.

It struck senior players that he had more than a streak of immaturity in his personality. During his period as captain he tended to gather the younger players round him. It puzzled me that he seemed to confide in them more than the seniors. This attitude was not ideal for a good team spirit.

My 1981–82 tour to Australia was without doubt my unhappiest. So many things about it were wrong. There was often bad feeling between the Pakistan and Australian players. Simmering personal feelings didn't take long to come to the surface—by the first Test, Dennis Lillee and Miandad were involved in an incident seen by millions on television and generally considered to be one of the unpleasantest in the history of international cricket. I shall have more to say about that a little later. Apart from psychological anxieties for me, I was in considerable pain for a great deal of the time after a delivery from Jeff Thomson which had cracked against my rib cage. The dressing room, I have to admit, was tense. Everything was boiling up to the open rebellion of the senior players and the claim from the hierarchy that we had refused to cooperate with Javed.

Oh yes, and it was an unreasonably demanding tour in the physical sense. This caused our manager Ijaz Butt to make an official complaint about the taxing schedule. 'Players,' he said, for everyone to hear and inwardly digest, 'need to be treated as human beings.'

Mr Butt was speaking at the end of the three-month tour. We had lost the Test series two–one to Australia and narrowly lost to them for a place in the finals for the one-day series. He spoke of the way his players were expected to switch techniques for Test and one-day matches. 'Chopping and changing all over a big country like Australia just isn't any good for a player's ability to produce his best. Players will soon start objecting to being treated as financial bait. They want to be treated as human beings.'

Most of us agreed with that. Our eyes were heavy and we were more than ready to go home and see our families. There were, as you may remember, more crises ahead.

But I must take it in stages—and that goes back to the 1981 season with Gloucestershire in England.

It is perhaps important to record, on the evidence of those closest to me at the time, that I was changing just a little as a person. For years I had been the quiet one, the cricketer who accepted orders without question: the meek mouse, if you like. I was never argumentative. If strong words were being exchanged in the dressing room, I chose to stay my distance.

Around the boundary at Bristol or Cheltenham, the supporters used to say: 'Zed's no trouble. He seems such an easygoing bloke.'

And so I still was, I liked to think. At the same time, I knew I was maturing. That meant I was beginning to question things more in my own mind. I was assuming an added element of independence. Maybe Packer had made me a little tougher, a little more analytical.

As I waited to bat or as I lay awake at night on away trips, I would say to myself: 'Come on, Zed, the records show you are one of Pakistan's most successful batsmen and in England you have some statistics that compare favourably with the great Wally Hammond. You have every right to assert yourself a little more.'

In that frame of mind I sent a letter from my home in Bristol to the cricket authorities in Pakistan. I told them I was batting at No. 4 now for Gloucestershire and succeeding there. It seemed the right place in the order for me now, I wrote, and that was where I wished to be considered for the forthcoming tour of Australia.

By my standards it was almost daring, although the request was surely reasonable enough. I received back a telex message in confirmation.

Off I went at the end of the English season, convinced that

44

from now on I would be batting at No. 4 or 5 for Pakistan. With the exception of one-day matches my career as a No. 3 was definitely over. I had no doubts about it—and I fully expected the chairman of selectors to accept that my mind was made up. But I was in for an embarrassing surprise. The chairman said he knew nothing of my recently declared preference to bat lower in the order. This mystified me after the trouble I had taken to notify the authorities in advance.

It came to the first meeting which I attended as the vice-captain. I asked what the batting line-up would be and was told unequivocably that I was first wicket down. 'But,' I protested, 'I have made my wishes very clear and the whole world knows them.' The response was that there was no-one else to do the job. The manager, Ijaz Butt, in particular was very emphatic.

This was no way to start an important tour. I left that meeting wondering whether my letter from England had been a complete waste of time. Who had seen it? Wasn't anyone prepared to take any notice of it? Did a civilised request from a senior player count for nothing?

The opening match was at Perth against Western Australia. I batted at No. 3 and made 24. I also remember that Majid hit a century and Javed used nine bowlers, everyone but myself and the wicket keeper.

I was again at No. 3 when we went on to Brisbane for the next game. Javed scored a century. My other memories are mixed—I hit 84 off the Queensland attack and was thumped on the ribs by Thompson. It didn't hurt too much at the time and I went on batting. But the pain increased, I was examined by a doctor and sent for an X-ray. By the next morning I was very sore indeed.

Javed was not playing in the following fixture against Victoria at Melbourne and I was due to captain the tourists. It was a cold, wet day when I reported to the ground. My ribs were throbbing and I knew I was in no state to play a game of cricket. Doctors had already told me I needed rest. I discussed my injury with some of the other players and left the ground.

What happened next was one of the most humiliating experiences of my life.

Back in the team hotel at Melbourne I curled up and tried to sleep. Then the 'phone went. It was to tell me in no uncertain terms that Javed wanted to see me.

'But what for?'

'He's annoyed with you for leaving the ground.'

'Everyone knows I'm not fit to play. One doctor told me to take three weeks off. If I try to play, it will make things worse.'

'Javed is the captain and he's summoning you. At the ground. Now.'

I was already displeased about statements Javed had given out to the Pakistan papers about my ability to carry on. Now this young man was ordering me to the ground.

I rinsed my mouth out, brushed my hair and rather angrily obeyed the summons. When I reached the ground, I sent a message that he should see me upstairs. I was after all very much senior to him and it seemed appropriate that this was a delicate matter to discuss in private.

Javed had other ideas. He made it clear that what he had to say would be expressed publicly in front of the rest of the team. He wanted me to come downstairs. I cannot possibly tell you how embarrassed I felt.

It was like an inquisition and I was a naughty schoolboy. He wanted to know why, as captain for the match, I had left the ground. I got the impression that he was making the scene deliberately in front of the boys in the team.

'You know, everyone in the team knows,' I blurted out, 'that I'm in no position to bat for the next three weeks.'

'You may have to bat for us here at Melbourne.'

'That's ridiculous. This isn't a Test match. If you lose this game, it isn't that important.'

A public row between a captain and his vice-captain is no way to start a tour. I fidgeted uneasily. So did some of the senior players who shared my embarrassment.

The record books show that although I was nominated as skipper I was 'absent hurt'. I didn't field or bat.

This quite unnecessary episode, in the presence of junior as well as senior players, was I should say the most distasteful in my whole career as a professional cricketer. It could have turned into a slanging match. I felt I showed remarkable restraint considering I had been wakened from my sleep.

The Test match was coming up. One doctor said he thought I should be able to play if I took pain-killer injections and had other treatment. It was even suggested that I should sleep with hot-water bottles to ease the pain. But I knew I couldn't possibly go through the motions of Test cricket. There was some criticism of me in the Pakistan papers, implying that I could play if I wanted to. This was hurtful.

In that November Test at Perth, Pakistan were all out for 62 in the first innings. We lasted for a rather shameful 21.3 overs. Sarfraz, going in at No. 8, was top score with 26.

My return to Pakistan was discussed. Javed talked about it to Imran, a good friend of mine. The version of that conversation I received was that if I was sent home I would be a hero—the Test had been lost and I hadn't played!

One moment I was on the point of being handed my passport, the next I was still—cracked ribs or not—very much a member of the touring side. Attitudes had changed.

I have already hinted at a decidedly cool fellow-feeling between the Australians and ourselves. No-one should have been too surprised by that. But few could have anticipated the way matters erupted in the infamous clash between Lillee and Javed. Columns of newsprint were devoted to it. Editorials were written and almost everyone disapproved of the behaviour of the fast bowler.

I may have been out of the Test side for that match at Perth but I saw everything that happened. It was unseemly and embarrassing. I have no doubt at all that Lillee aimed his kick at Javed quite deliberately. Later he came into our dressing room and apologised, implying at the same time that our skipper had been doing 'funny things' to him. Personal animosities are not new in first class cricket and no doubt there had been exchanges on the field between the two of them. For Lillee to react in that way to a visiting captain in front of the public was inexcusable. Some of our players made it clear to him.

At the time the Australian bowler was edging towards his world record for wicket-taking. He has never been renowned for a quiet manner or an abundance of good taste. I don't think the criticisms bother him too much; he knows no-one will take his wonderful career record away from him.

But he made a world-wide television audience cringe at Perth. Some of his own team-mates, used to a saga of dubious behaviour from Lillee, agreed that he had gone too far this time. His past contretemps with Mike Brearley were bad enough. So were his publicity-seeking antics with an aluminium bat. Now there was an element of physical violence, however restrained— and many were none too sure it was particularly restrained.

He had to be suspended, of course. Our manager Ijaz Butt approved of the prompt action and diplomatically said that as far as the Pakistan Board were concerned, the matter was now closed.

Henry Blofeld, the well-known broadcaster and journalist, wrote in *The Cricketer*:

> I very much doubt if there has ever been a more unpleasant incident in a Test match than that at Perth when Lillee first deliberately blocked the Pakistan captain as he was completing a single and then launched a kick at him when he had made his crease. Over the years Lillee has been involved in probably more unpleasant incidents than any other Test cricketer. He has seemed almost to make a habit of trying to bait and upset his opponents in the most petulant manner.

It was hardly surprising that Javed appeared to lose his temper. He lifted his bat as though ready to strike Lillee if he contemplated another kick. Back in the pavilion we held our breath. It was a very nasty moment and had little to do with a game of cricket.

The umpire at the bowler's end, Tony Crafter, sensed the likelihood of more trouble. He jumped in front of Lillee. Meanwhile the Australian's skipper, Greg Chappell, was chasing up from slip to help take the steam out of a ghastly situation. I hope I shall never see anything like this on a cricket field again.

Our manager wasted no time in making an official protest to the chairman of the Australian Cricket Board, Phil Ridings, who after all had been present and seen at first hand the show of

48

antipathy between two international players.

When we heard just how seriously Lillee's fellow players viewed the incident—under the new disciplinary structure they self-consciously imposed an almost token fine of £120—members and officials of the Pakistan party felt angry and slighted. It was patently inadequate and the two-match ban that followed, carrying with it a substantial loss in wages, went some way towards placating the more vociferous critics of Lillee in the Pakistan dressing room.

The official statement from the Australian Board contained some ambiguities. Lillee and a number of the Australian players maintained vehemently that the bowler never blocked Javed. They argued that our captain could have avoided Lillee but chose deliberately to strike him 'with bat and body'. Their case was that Lillee retaliated after being struck! The umpires saw things differently and they claimed that Javed's path was blocked as he completed his run.

It takes two to make a row and no-one would have suggested that the relationship of Lillee and Javed was ever especially cordial. On the last day of that traumatic Test, Lillee came into our dressing room. He was in no mood to make too many concessions. He apologised but left us in no doubt that he considered he was provoked.

Javed did not accept the apology. There was no hand-shake or apparent effort to patch up a bitter clash that threatened to take up as much space on the front pages as our historic Partition.

Maybe our somewhat temperamental captain mellowed a little. Later in the series he was quoted as saying: 'I was very disappointed about what happened and felt sorry for Dennis—in his testimonial year. That thing was just one or two seconds when we lost our tempers. You don't think of the consequences at a time like that.'

As captain, Miandad was frequently being quoted—in the Australian papers and home in Pakistan. Some of the statements he made did not exactly please me, as you will have gathered. But there were lighter moments to offset the overall gloom of the tour.

I am thinking of the misinterpreted remark of his that so upset Greg Chappell.

49

'He completely misunderstood. I had shouted out: "Faqih, you've got him in three." Chappell obviously thought I had sworn at him and he told me to watch it!'

That chance remark, centred round the name of Ejaz Faqih has, I understand, been the basis of a score of after-dinner stories round the world ...

Equally amusing, among those who knew him best, was Lillee's indignant remark that he might retire from cricket altogether if he were suspended. The fiercely outspoken and impulsive Aussie would never have parted company with an imminent bowling record that easily.

When his anger had subsided, he even said in an unguarded moment: 'Now it's time to get on with the cricket again.'

You could say that again. Personally I set about that very task with as much enthusiasm as I could muster. I was still in pain from my damaged ribs. From the second day of the tour I had known that I should be wretchedly unhappy. The chemistry was all wrong; at times you could cut the atmosphere with a knife. I retreated into a shell and became depressed. Yet above all I desperately wanted to regain complete fitness and to start scoring runs for Pakistan again.

The first of the Benson and Hedges World Series Cup matches was due in a few days' time. I was examined by the doctors again and tried running around in my bedroom at the hotel. I still felt pain although it wasn't as severe. I told my captain: 'Please don't announce the team till the last minute. I'm not 100 per cent fit but I'll try to play if you want me to.'

When the rest of the boys in the team knew that I was prepared to return I could see that they were very happy. For my part I agreed to bat at No. 3, as this was a one-day match.

I found myself captaining Pakistan in several of the matches in this Cup series. At Sydney, I scored a century against the Australians; I was top score in four other matches, two of them against the fiery West Indies attack.

I had come back for the second official Test in the late November at Brisbane. We lost by ten wickets, a result hardly likely to endear us to our more critical supporters at home. At No. 5, I made 80 in the first innings after we had been sent in to bat.

Everyone had imagined that the bad spirit from the first Test would be carried over. That was not strictly true. Despite burning ears and some resentment about public criticism, Tony Crafter and Mel Johnson were again the umpires. Miandad and Lillee restricted the bitterness of recent experiences to glaring at each other down the length of the wicket. The snorting Australian seemed predictably unforgiving. His first ball at our captain was dug in short. It kicked up and hit the batsman's left shoulder. First blood to Lillee. When Javed played on to Lillee, the bowler's expression was that of a proud conqueror.

We won the final Test by an innings—and lost the series. Again I succeeded with an innings of 90. Perhaps it isn't too immodest of me, in view of the traumatic background and my injuries, which were a good deal less mythical than a few unkind people were implying, that I came out on top of the Test averages (56.66). Javed Miandad was second (41) and Wasim Raja (36.20) third.

Our young captain appeared to relish the opportunity to express strong words to the media. He was not afraid to arraign his players.

Some of us smarted for a long time after his crushing words when we lost the second Test. I can understand his disappointment; we were two down in the series and there would be no triumphant return to Pakistan. And indeed some of our batting in the second innings at Brisbane had been inept.

Javed went on record as saying some of the players ignored his instructions to play for a draw on the final day when we were 157 runs behind but had all our wickets in hand. I know I was out to a bad shot and was full of self-reproof when I returned to the dressing room.

'Our senior players,' said Javed, with me no doubt in mind, 'went for runs when I felt we could have saved the match.' He was very cross about it. While he turned on us, he seemed to hold out an olive branch to the abrasive and flamboyant Lillee, who had after all taken 4–51 to put the series ruthlessly out of our reach. 'Lillee was fantastic,' he said. It was a fair and brave assessment. Lillee bowled marvellously and was now, I remember, just four wickets short of Lance Gibbs' record Test haul.

On and off the field, the division between our captain and most of his senior players had grown. I recall saying to him on one occasion: 'I have cooperated with you, batting when not fully fit and going in at No. 3 for some of the matches. But you have simply not cooperated with me.'

Tours are not easy. They call for give-and-take and, in some cases, a selfless pooling of personalities. If the captain chooses to side primarily with the young members of the party, factions are bound to develop.

Rebels and Rancour

There was some good cricket in between. Centuries from Miandad, Majid and Rizwan-uz-Zaman; Mudassar missed out by five in the third Test, Imran was seven short in another match; Qasim and Imran took most wickets. Statisticians pointed out that Javed and myself set up a new fourth-wicket record stand (128) for Pakistan against Australia in the Melbourne Test. I know that Majid became only the second Pakistan batsman to play 100 Test innings (Mushtaq was the other).

I am aware that the more cynical observers of the cricket scene are inclined to say that Pakistan seem to attract controversy. Well, I have to concede that it was painfully so for much of that 1981–82 tour to Australia.

When Majid fell over someone's feet in the dressing room as he waited his turn to bat, and injured his back, we knew that our luck was out!

I have charted the differences within our team at some length because it would be absurd and dishonest to pretend that we went through the motions of enjoying our cricket in Australia. We flew home to Pakistan and, figuratively and literally, rebellion was in the air.

The Pakistan Cricket Board confirmed that Javed Miandad would again be captain—for the coming Test series against Sri Lanka and then our 1982 visit to England. Most of us were shocked and dismayed. The decision, announced by the Board president, Air Marshall Nur Khan, was said to have been unanimous. In a news conference, the president made it clear that the Board's general council had discussed the growing crisis within the team.

53

What was that unprecedented crisis? Only that ten players were at one point not prepared to make themselves available for any Test team led by Javed.

The ten were Majid Khan, Imran Khan, Wasim Raja, Sarfraz Nawaz, Mudassar Nazir, Iqbal Qasim, Mohsin Khan, Sikandar Bakht, Wasim Bari and myself.

Back in Pakistan the telephone wires were busy between Lahore and Karachi. We held meetings and most of us remained emphatic that we must not give way. Meanwhile the Board were saying that they were ready to give the rebels the chance still to play 'without any loss of face' and they claimed that several were keen to return to the fold.

Apart from general dissatisfaction about the climate and lack of rapport in Australia between the captain and his players, we were by this time very sensitive about allegations that some of us had openly refused to cooperate with Javed on tour. We issued a statement: 'Since it is of the utmost importance that there should be confidence and cooperation among the captain and the team members, the allegations have generated an uneasy feeling about Javed Miandad's ability to lead the team.'

Impasse. People were asking whether this was an unacceptable show of player-power. Who would give way? Could Pakistan's board risk a permanent rift with its most gifted cricketers?

There was an emergency meeting of the general council of the Board. Players came face to face with Nur Khan; feelings were made very clear. The Board set a deadline for the rebels prepared to toe the line.

Our intransigence should have surprised no-one. The upshot was that we were 'dropped' for the first Test against Sri Lanka in Karachi. But by now the replacement team included Wasim Raja and Iqbal Qasim.

Almost daily, the bizarre business took a new, unhappy twist. Ijaz Butt, the chairman of selectors, resigned as a protest against what he reasonably termed 'the disintegration of cricket in Pakistan'. He suggested that the president was too rigid in his attitude. Majid was acting as our spokesman and he pointed out that we were ready to play under Javed in the Sri Lanka matches but not in England. By now the rebels were said to be down to seven. Mohsin Khan was stated by Majid to be under pressure from his employers. The new chief selector was named as Maqsood Ahmed.

It may be difficult for outsiders to realise the unanimity of the remaining rebels. We considered we had logic and a principle on our side and there would be no shifting. As a consequence we missed the first two Tests and were accepted back for the third at Lahore, where we won by an innings and I gained some personal satisfaction by scoring 134. Pakistan had actually won the first Test and drawn the second.

Before that third Test, Javed made a statement in which he said he would not be available to captain his country in England during 1982. He was standing down, he said, in the interests of his country and he hoped that the seven rebel players would now be available for the last Sri Lanka Test and for the remaining one-day internationals.

Javed's statement gave new hopes all round. The chance of his still going to England as an ordinary playing member of the tour party was not ruled out.

In retrospect we can only regret that a fierce domestic cricket row in Pakistan was emblazoned in such an undignified way around the world. We are not ashamed of the stand we took and we hope that good has come from it. I can only report that team spirit in England during the summer of 1982 was refreshingly high. The senior players got on well with Javed.

Well, was there an element of unyielding player-power? The measured words of Intikhab are of value. He was once a capable and intelligent captain himself; more recently he has proved an admirable manager. And he believes Pakistan has suffered from 'a gap in communications'.

I share that feeling. At the end of the Australian tour every member gave a report and there were some caustic comments about the captaincy. I simply signed the form.

Now that whole unsavoury chapter belongs to the past. I felt I needed to put it on paper as a kind of therapy. I like to think everyone—Board and players—benefited. The signs are good.

There will always be occasions when players have to take on,

Just a face in the crowd. Zaheer had been playing for Kerry Packer and was flown back to Karachi for what might have been an unscheduled Test appearance against England in 1978.

(Photograph *Patrick Eagar*)

however reluctantly, a militant character. And I am thinking back farther than the series, when Sarfraz made his own pointed and dramatic stand over expenses!

The pay for representing your country at cricket in Pakistan used to be appalling. That, I promise you, was not just my opinion. When I started playing, during the days when Abdul Hafeez Kardar was in charge, I would receive 150 rupees for a match. Much more recently, with an overdue realism, I got 9,000 rupees (about £450). I leave you to work out what it used to be—but it was a shameful reward for Test recognition.

One of the first English words I learned when I switched from Urdu was 'peanuts'. Everyone in the Pakistan team told me it summed up our wages.

Eventually the grievances of the players spilled over into open revolt. We reached the ground late for a Test match at Hyderabad and made it clear that we were not prepared to play unless payments improved. I felt at the time—and still do—that the method was too drastic. But I considered I had a duty to lend my support.

What else is there to be said about the Kerry Packer revolution? Once, not so many years ago, it was the most sensational development in sport. Pads and balls changed colour; establishment feathers were ruffled; the lawyers made money. Now the headlines and the court cases are almost forgotten.

How shall I remember it? There's no doubt in my mind—my abiding memory is of the day when Pakistan selected a Test side of 23 players. You will never beat that. It was funny and sad at the same time.

I was part of Packer cricket. It was a bold, imaginative, fearless plan by an Australian entrepreneur who was not afraid to take on some of the game's fuddy-duddies. He did not encourage disloyalty. In the case of the Pakistan players, for instance, he was anxious for us to serve our countries and made it easy for us to do so. That, initially, we were not wanted is another story altogether.

Enough words have already been written about World Series Cricket and the philosophy behind it. I have not once been diverted from my original conviction that it was a good and timely thing for cricket—and an undeniable benefit to many underpaid players. Just ask a few modest county cricketers in England. They were never going to be talented enough to join Mr Packer; but the salaries increased as an indirect result of his dramatic intervention.

I was playing in a county match at Hampshire when I received a phone call from the Dorchester Hotel in London. The scheme was briefly and discreetly outlined to me. 'Might you be interested, Zaheer?'

'Interested? I'd love it.'

Word of the Australia-based circus had already vaguely reached me on the grapevine. The prospect of competing with and against the greatest players in the world—and being paid handsomely for it—was an exciting thought.

I can't say the ethics came into it. My first reaction was that this was an enterprising way of sharpening up my reflexes at the crease in a showcase situation.

I realised the need for discretion. When I was invited to the Dorchester myself, the details were set out for me and contracts were mentioned for the first time. They made me whistle.

Other prominent Pakistan players had been approached. I saw no reason to start worrying how the Board might respond. I was in England, playing cricket for Gloucestershire. Board members were a long way away at Lahore. The distance blurred any consideration of the consequences.

In no time at all, of course, I found myself along with Mushtaq and Asif, Majid and Imran, almost an outcast. Like all the other players who had signed for Mr Packer, we were stunned by the hostile and even hysterical reaction to our so-called defection.

The Board took its traditional rigid stand. Its members were pleased with the way Pakistan were gaining stature as a cricketing country. Now, with what so many people apparently saw as an act of treason, Test sides were being disrupted and new divisions were being created.

Sarfraz, Javed and Haroon Rashid joined us. While we all adapted ourselves to the new techniques and learned to ride the insults of those who disapproved of our action, a weakened Pakistan Test side, captained by Wasim Bari, played out three draws. During that uninspiring series, my relatives and friends at home kept me informed of the confusion and conflicting rumours about our likely return to welcoming arms.

There were certainly positive efforts to bring us back, whatever the trend of world opinion. According to a report in *Wisden*: 'The first intimation that practical steps were being taken to include "Packerstanis" for the first Test at Lahore came briefly on the radio when the touring England team were in faraway Peshawar, the frontier town at the gateway to the Khyber Pass. It was surprising news to Imtiaz Ahmed, the Pakistan chairman of selectors, who was attending the match.'

The authorities actually made contact with Mushtaq in Australia. They must have taken an unduly optimistic view because on the strength of it they named 23 players from whom the Test side would be chosen. I hope sports editors had space to list all of us. It must have been intriguing and highly comical.

Put it down to wise counsel or a lack of communication—take your pick—but we never left Australia. When it came to the third Test, however, at Karachi, everyone appeared to know that Mushtaq, Imran and myself were on our way. Mr Kerry had given his blessing.

The England players and officials were not amused. Telex messages rattled away to Douglas Insole, chairman of the Test and County Cricket Board, and its secretary Donald Carr. The players held heated meetings and bluntly said they did not want to play against Packer representatives. Some of the Pakistan team, who had played in the first two Tests and welcomed the additional scope, were equally antagonistic to us. Mushtaq, Imran and myself got on with our net practice at Karachi. We left others to do the theorising and make political judgments.

Bob Willis, later to become England's captain and very much an establishment figure in some ways, was one of our sternest critics at the time.

Not that all of us feel that Bob, fine fast bowler that he is, has always been one of our best friends. His coldly off-hand treatment of Iqbal Qasim at Edgbaston in 1978 apparently lost him rather a lot of fans in Pakistan. I read about the way Willis let fly a bouncer at Iqbal who had come in as night-watchman and had been doing uncommonly well for his side for 40 minutes or so. The ball hit the batsman with a sickening thud and what upset everyone—not least many in England—was that Willis showed a complete lack of concern. He actually said later that his concentration would have suffered if he had seen the blood.

I don't approve of his action that day against a low-order batsman. Nor do I approve of some of his remarks that have gone into print about our involvement in Packer:

> The Pakistan Board had in a statement bristling with righteous indignation talked disparagingly about Kerry Packer who had shown 'complete disregard to the entire cricket establishment.' The principle that Packer players should remain outside the Test fold was strongly underlined in January 1978. But there followed a disastrous tour by their weakened side and to no-one's astonishment, seven Packer players were back in the team for the prestigious series against India. The clash of ideals did not matter to either the Board or the players. Pakistan won the Lahore Test and what could be more important to them than beating India.

Of the Karachi match, to which three Packer players had flown, Willis commented pungently: 'We resented the implication that Kerry Packer was running the show . . . Eventually the Pakistan Board made a statement which pointed out that the Packer men would not play the next day. They had arrived of their own accord and had refused to apologise for making themselves unavailable for Tests.'

The opinionated Willis went on to wonder whether the England players would have withdrawn from the game if myself and the other Packer rebels had been selected.

He has said that the whole incident deepened his disenchantment with Pakistani cricket—and it hardly lessened when in the final Test of that edgy series England had half a dozen LBWs against them in the first innings. Several, he claimed, were dubious. What is that I have heard about Pakistani players whining about umpires' decisions?

It would be wrong to say we were insensitive to some of the things said about us. There was a lack of balance in the comment. The sheer hypocrisy has been brought home to me by the way the erstwhile rebel players who dared to join Packer and his 'cricket by floodlight' have eventually been welcomed back by their countries and counties as though they don't know what all the fuss was about.

In October 1977, *The Cricketer* reprinted an editorial from the Pakistan *Times* which read: 'While it is difficult to visualise a Pakistan side without Majid Khan, Mushtaq Mohammad, Zaheer Abbas, and Imran Khan, it is equally difficult to understand what can only be called their indecent avarice ... there is no doubt that Packer started on the wrong foot and now he and the professionals are trying to plead the kind of piety of which they have shown themselves incapable throughout the last months ...'

Cricket writer Z. H. Syed claimed: 'Another development of the present controversy is the complete lack of sympathy on the part of the general public for those Pakistan players who signed for Packer. This is a contrast with the situation in October 1976 when almost everybody supported their demands for better pay scales.'

But in a later editorial, the Pakistan *Times* took a more liberal view of our defection: 'The element of self-righteousness that has characterised the BCCP's handling of the whole affair cannot be appreciated. The fact is that at least three of the cricketers signified their willingness to play for Pakistan if that did not clash with their commitments to Packer—which meant the first two Tests against England. If the BCCP had adopted a more moderate attitude, maybe the players might have been induced to go along a little farther. It was not a question of kow-towing to anybody but merely trying to win back stars to the fold. As it is, we have been left with a weak side. It is not easy entirely to shake off the feeling that if bad blood had not been created by the BCCP over the fees issue prior to the Hyderabad Test against New Zealand last year, the situation might have been different today.'

I have been told of the demonstrations that took place during the unsuccessful three-match series against England. There are many Pakistanis living in England; others made a special journey. They were openly antagonistic to the Pakistan Board and handed out leaflets. They didn't hide their admiration for the Packer players.

Perhaps we should be grateful for their loyalty. But it was unfortunate that they should turn on the weakened Test team instead.

What ultimately happened is now history. We were brought back to help defeat India. By the March of 1979 we were playing for Pakistan again—this time against an Australia team *without* its Packer men. It was all a little confusing and some people became rather cynical. I was grateful when things got back quickly to normal.

A Joke That Went Too Far

As long as I can remember, umpires have had a rough time of it. They accept that criticism of the way they do their job is an occupational hazard.

A Test series rarely goes by without a few umpiring controversies. Our manager and skipper, Inti and Imran had penetrative words to say about some of the decisions during the matches in England in 1982. That was their prerogative.

It isn't a one-way campaign and I recall the English players huffing and puffing about umpiring standards in India and Pakistan.

I should hate to be an umpire. The degree of concentration is too intense—and I could not risk getting wet through too often. Perhaps I should explain myself. It goes back to early 1956 when I was only eight years old.

England were engaged on the third unofficial Test at Peshawar on the North West frontier. There was an official dinner to the two teams on the Sunday. Just before midnight one of the umpires was ... kidnapped.

It sounds like a joke. Instead it became an international incident. There was talk of cancelling the tour and reimbursing Pakistan for loss of receipts. Meetings at high-diplomacy level were held and abject apologies were extended. Never has a cricketing nation eaten such humble pie. I read about it and heard it discussed by my family. Everyone seemed to be discussing it. No-one quite knew whether to laugh or cry.

The circumstances remain fresh in my memory. This is what happened on a sultry Sunday night when the England players should have been thinking of bed and the current Test match.

One of the umpires, Idris Begh, had gone back from the official dinner to his hotel. He was planning to go to bed when a number of the England players suddenly arrived, 'captured' him and bundled him into a tonga, or horse-drawn carriage. Several of them were wearing handkerchiefs, giving the impression of comic gangsters. They drove Mr Begh back to their hotel where, in one of the player's rooms, he had water poured over him.

With a remarkable show of tact, he later told journalists: 'I am quite ready to enter into the spirit of a rag but this went beyond that. I hear the MCC are proposing disciplinary steps against Donald Carr's men and I hope the authorities are not too severe on them. By the tone of their apology I can see they are full of regrets for over-stepping the mark. I still count the Englishmen among my friends!'

That wasn't the end of his surprisingly good nature. When the MCC side were eventually defeated, they were jeered off the field and left the ground under police protection. That was what the spectators thought of the so-called prank. Mr Begh appealed to the crowd 'not to insult Pakistan's guests.'

I don't pretend to know what possessed a group of supposedly mature international cricketers, briefed in advance no doubt on the virtues of good behaviour in a foreign country, to indulge in an undergraduate-style joke of dubious taste. Surely they were intelligent enough to imagine what the outcome might be.

Our papers thundered in protest. The British journals were just as sweeping in their condemnation. The late Peter Wilson, one of the most famous sports writers in England, wrote:

> When the MCC sends a team representing this country abroad we are entitled to *hope* that they will win but to *expect* that they will at least behave with dignity and propriety. This was some of the most oafish behaviour that I have ever come across in international sport ... Unless there are extenuating circumstances, which I find hard to imagine, I hope the MCC will act rapidly and drastically.

The incident, which was alleged to have involved an attempt to persuade Mr Begh, a Moslem, to take some alcohol, became one of diplomatic embarrassment. The Governor-General, Major

General Iskander Mirza, also president of the Cricket Board, received a visit from Group Captain Cheema, the Board secretary. The MCC manager Geoffrey Howard called on the wronged umpire and the Pakistan captain, Hafeez Kardar, as he was then known.

Apologies were actually flying around only hours after the late-night prank. There was bland, unconvincing talk that the incident was closed and everyone would pretend it had never happened. I read that the day after the kidnapping, a cocktail party was given for the two teams by the British Deputy High Commissioner. Not a single Pakistan player turned up.

Back in London, the MCC president Lord Alexander fired off a succession of cables, offering his personal apologies.

Nothing could have been more untimely that the manhandling of the Test umpire. There had been consistent rumblings about the standard of umpiring. Jim Parks was the victim of one bad mistake which even brought a message of regret from our authorities. Imtiaz Ahmed had complained about the bad language directed at him by an MCC player.

Ah well, things have not changed so very much after all. You should hear the language when we take on Dennis Lillee and co.

Even back in 1956 it was being proposed that neutral umpires should be used. In the later summer of 1982 I heard our manager Intikhab calling for a panel of neutral umpires, and Imran suggesting that it might make sense for independent assessors to sit in the stand behind the bowler's arm.

As a cricketing nation we are being continually accused of making life intolerable for the umpires. Our critics say that we are far too noisy: that we appeal for everything, often from a position in the field where it is totally impossible to judge the line of the ball, and that we show dissent when decisions go against us. If the rather sneaky implication is that we are cheats, we refute it with some passion. I don't happen to be an exuberant person and you will not often see me expressing extravagant emotions in the field. But, for the most part, Pakistan players are excitable. We collectively accept no blame for displaying our enthusiasm. If the bowler, wicket keeper and close fielders rise in unison as they ask for a catch, that is the *professional* response of a team believing that they have earned a success.

These same critics argue that our abrasive relationship with umpires goes back a long way, years before our displeasure with Tony Crafter and Mel Johnson in Australia. And they say that we became insufferable during the 1982 England series.

Perhaps I should make my personal statement first of all. I was on the receiving end of a questionable LBW decision when facing Botham in the final Test. It came when I was trying so hard to shake off the effects of ill health and to make some timely runs in a match which could have gone either way. Quietly I discussed my dismissal with my manager. Some of my colleagues were convinced I was not out. I must say, in honesty, that the decision rather surprised me.

But it has never been my policy to whine about the standard of umpiring. By the law of averages, every umpire is bound to make the occasional bad judgment. None of them do it deliberately.

From the time I first arrived in England, I found umpires as a breed extremely helpful to me. I have no complaints. The standard of umpiring in England is, I believe, the best in the world.

If the volatile approach of some of our players puts an added pressure on the umpires we would retort that cricket is an emotional game—especially for Pakistanis—and we do nothing illegally.

Our leg-spinner Abdul Qadir was pilloried because, in the words of Denis Compton, now a cricket writer, 'he went into a war-dance of rage' when David Constant turned down an LBW appeal against Ian Botham. Javed was similarly mocked for drop-kicking the ball at Edgbaston in a show of exasperation.

Come on, England! Are some of your actions on the field so immune from criticism?

Most of us have seen Botham indicating to the opposing batsman in fairly unambiguous fashion, after taking a wicket, the nearest route to the pavilion. We have all seen Robin Jackman's emotional approach to the art of bowling. On the county circuit in England, I quickly discovered the sides who were better shouters than batters. It never remotely bothered me.

66

I am told that we lost some friends during the 1982 summer by the way we hammered away at the umpires. Most of the criticism was voiced by our manager and captain. They were the people in authority to do that. I should add that Inti, a quiet, wise man who made an unqualified success of the job he took on as manager at a delicate stage in our cricket history, chooses his words with care. He has considerable integrity. If he is asked a question he will answer it as honestly as he can. He does not shirk controversial issues; he has a great loyalty to his team and will defend them in public.

Imran, a dashing figure and an inspiring leader, is equally perceptive. He is a fearless cricketer and has an appropriately intrepid attitude towards making the kind of statements that he feels are called for. By an odd twist he found himself leading a side which had three former Pakistan skippers, cousin Majid, Wasim Bari and Miandad. This never inhibited him—and the players approved of the way he spoke out.

There were complaints about the umpires in all three Tests. Ken Palmer and David Evans were accused of being inconsistent in their handling of the first. Inti was quite emphatic that the balance of decisions went against us. He thought there were up to half a dozen doubtful decisions.

This stung Palmer, a former Somerset all-rounder, into a reply. He chose to overstate in his defence. 'If we'd given Pakistan everything they asked for, England would have been out for single figures in each innings. They obviously expect a favourable decision on all their appeals but when 99 per cent are ridiculous and turned down, life becomes difficult if not impossible for umpires.'

I can only say that many English spectators and TV watchers were ready to say that mistakes were made.

By the time we got to the third Test, David Constant—removed from the panel of umpires for the series against India earlier—and Barrie Meyer were being subjected to our criticism. The dismissal of Sikander, for an alleged catch, was a bit of a shocker. We watched it back on television and there must have been a case for the commentators to express an opinion. They do, after all, when an LBW is given.

Imran left no-one in any doubt about his feelings. This is what he said immediately after the third Test. 'I'm not making excuses—it's the last thing I want to do after being beaten. But I was disappointed with the umpiring in the series. It was not intentional, of course, and I don't believe that umpires cheat anywhere in the world. But David Constant cost us the match. Everybody knew that David Gower had been caught behind in the first innings when he was on seven. He started to walk but stood his ground when he was given not out, and went on to make 74. Then came the decision against Sikander. I was at the other end and couldn't believe it.'

He softened his remarks by going on to say, just as I do, that the English umpires are the world's best. When someone asked him whether there was too much appealing, he denied that this was done to put pressure on the umpire. 'It's up to them to stand firm and make the right decision.'

I understand that Constant and Meyer would have liked the opportunity to answer the charges against them and that other umpires were getting increasingly worried about the public criticisms, whether from India or Pakistan.

The TCCB allowed no right of reply and, whatever the merits of the umpires, that seemed undemocratic to me.

It is healthy to air grievances. Surely we had a legitimate one back in 1974 when we played against England at Lord's.

We considered that the wicket had been covered with dreadful inadequacy. Rain had conveniently seeped through the covers. And where do you think that ominous damp patch was? Bang on the spot for Derek Underwood.

Are you surprised that the Pakistan boys gave each other long, wry looks—and that some pretty pointed remarks were made publicly?

Underwood took 6–9 and although he got me for one in each innings it isn't a question of sour grapes. Some rebukes to those responsible for covering Test wickets were rightly made. If the match hadn't ended in a draw—thanks to more rain—I suspect our statements would have contained even more brimstone.

In the context of controversy—over the eventful, if brief, history of Pakistan cricket—I turn at last to the behaviour of our crowds.

68

The reputation is an unenviable one. There is a sorry chapter of disturbances, motivated by everything from political unrest to sheer boredom. Too often our matches have been enacted against a background of national unease—and one has affected the other. At times it has been unfortunate that a cricket match has been going on simultaneously.

Chair-fights, stone-throwing and ugly skirmishes with the police have been a predictable pattern, though the Cricket Board and of course the players earnestly hope that a new era of stability has arrived.

Although I wasn't yet a Test player, I still remember, with some dismay, what happened when England came to play three matches against us in 1969. The last, in my hometown of Karachi, eventually had to be abandoned because of rioting. That was the game when Colin Milburn was flown in from Western Australia and scored a century on his Test debut. He'd started in the style that made him such a favourite around the world until his sickening car crash. This happy, chubby figure came in and immediately started hitting cheeky boundaries off Asif Masood. The century couldn't have been a more popular one; the only trouble was that young supporters, over-excited in their recognition of his feat, streamed on to the field. There were several hundred of them and Tom Graveney, the other batsman, became rather concerned for Colin's safety. Without too much visible vigour, he tried to ward off some advancing pitch invaders. He found himself later accused of being too free with the use of his bat.

Tom, an idol of mine for his exquisite off-side strokes—he has made a new career for himself as a Test match commentator, when not looking after his pub in Gloucestershire—would joke with friends about that explosive Karachi match and his apparent involvement in it.

'Do you know, they weren't very hard but I reckon they were the only decent strokes I'd played up to then!'

The ground surrounds were overflowing with demonstrators, protesting about the political set-up as well as the Board's cricket selectors. There was a noisy lobby to bring back Hanif Mohammad as captain, I remember, in place of Saeed.

On the day before the finish, Alan Knott was going well and was four short of what would have been his first Test century. Then the rioting erupted again, the pitch was invaded and the match abandoned.

I don't know what the England players made of it. Some of the more militant students did not feel that the match should ever have started. In impassioned speeches they argued that the community should have their minds on the more pressing political issues of the day. The city was, I recall, in some turmoil at the time and teachers were on hunger-strike and many lives in Pakistan were being lost.

It was a strange, uneasy series, only arranged at the last moment. Colin Cowdrey was the captain and he must have read, on the 'plane journey out, of the troubles in East Pakistan, as it then was. There was a state of emergency and the part of the tour in the eastern section was cancelled.

At Lahore, where the first Test was played, the tourists must have quickly sensed the growing political agitation and the unpopularity of President Ayub Khan. The players found themselves in the direct line of the demonstrators and at one stage they cautiously locked themselves in at the Continental Hotel. When the cricket actually got started, armed military guards patrolled the boundary. Chairs and fruit were hurled at the police.

It wasn't quite Tunbridge Wells or Cheltenham in late August.

I don't intend to catalogue other crowd disturbances. A cricket pitch is a useful public platform if you have a political point you want to make. It is too bad if the players get in the way.

Elsewhere in this book I have said that I try to distance myself from politics. My father was a government employee and he could see the wisdom of expressing no strong views.

While the riots have gone on, slogans have been chanted and speeches made, I have sat helplessly on the grass or back in the pavilion with my team-mates. We have not been impervious to the distress and the bloodshed around Pakistan and often we have had some sympathy with the arguments of the de-monstrators. But we were after all paid to play cricket . . . and leave the politics and the nation's well-being to others.

Karachi holds so many sad memories. There is always trouble of some sort. The supporters can be over-demanding. They want their own way—they want to meet the players and to be seen on TV in the process. They want Pakistan to win. The girls come for our autographs and it looks bad if we don't give them. The boys are ruthless and persistent; they simply won't go away. How can you concentrate? There's little privacy for the players and someone is always walking in front of you as you wait your turn to bat.

This is not an attack on the National Stadium, where after all I have frequently done well and where I appreciate the warmth and kindness shown to me. But, in truth, I do not enjoy playing there. The crowds are altogether too fickle, a criticism which also applies to some other grounds in Pakistan. They slap us on the back and say: 'Well done, well done,' when we win something. At other times they throw stones and abuse us. How can I forget the day they turned against us and smashed the windows on the team coach. We sat pensively on the grass.

I am a proud Pakistani and I spiritually identify with much that has been achieved, maybe by unorthodox means, in the idealistic pursuit of progress and peace.

Yet at the same time I yearn for the quiet life, devoid of boundary riots, chair fights and hassle, even at the wicket.

In tranquil evenings at home, I place my daughters on my lap and look with eyes full of meaning to Najma. There is a peaceful contentment in surburban Karachi or Westbury-on-Trym, Bristol that comes as a blissful relief to me.

PRELIMINARIES

Father's Famous Escape Route

I was born less than a month before Partition. It wasn't the best of times—whatever the political advantages of the Great Divide.

Moslem and Hindu went his own way at midnight on 14 August 1947. My birth took place in the Punjab city of Sialkot on 24 July. I can only imagine the anxieties of my parents; I was their first baby and the circumstances of a nation, in the apprehensive throes of independence, kept my father and mother apart.

My father, Syed Ghulam Shabbir, was stationed at Bikanar in the middle of the Rajisthan Desert, forming part of Bharat (India). He was an employee of the Federal Government in the Locust Control Organisation. He had opted for service in the emerging Pakistan and was expected to report for duty in the country he had chosen. Sialkot was his home town, in the geographical and emotional sense.

My mother, Kaneez Fatima, came from a village called Shergarh, in the Sahiwal district of Punjab. They were married in 1943: a sensitive, intelligent, kindly couple who worried like so many about the traditional problems of their homeland, of religious differences, of illiteracy and poverty. They idealistically looked forward to the raising of children of whom, in the words of my father 'we could feel proud and content with the knowledge that we would be leaving behind a better generation.'

Partition was an exciting time—and a fearsome one. I have listened intently to what my father has told me about it. I have read of the horrifying teething troubles—of murder and destruction, of the way scores of villages were burned down, of the kidnapping of thousands of women and children. Centuries of hate seemed to boil over as Hindus, Moslems and Sikhs killed one another on a dreadful scale. By the following January Gandhi was dead, assassinated by a Hindu fanatic.

My father, a wise and protective man, had foreseen the mounting tensions that would accompany Partition. He ensured that my mother would stay in Sialkot in preparation for my birth. Father was later to reminisce: 'How dangerous her stay at my station of duty could have been is shown by the fact that the special train carrying Pakistan personnel from New Delhi to Karachi was bombed and derailed at Bhatinda on the night of 9 August and the Moslem occupants of subsequent trains destined for Pakistan border stations were massacred.' He had planned to come to the West Punjab, in Pakistan—via Bhatinda, East Punjab in India—to join his family. But he saw what was happening and took a different path.

In fact, he worked out that he had more or less followed the escape route of the Mogul king Humayur nearly 500 years ago. Humayur had been defeated by Sher Shah Suri and saved himself and his pregnant wife by entering the Tharparkar desert. By the time he got to Umerkot, on the western fringe of the desert—now part of Pakistan—there was an emergency stop. His refugee wife gave birth to Akbar. The Mogul dynasty became the outstanding one in Indian history. Akbar the Great was just 13 when he became king in 1556.

This book is in no way at all a history lesson. But I suspect that the similarity of my father's escape route with that of the great Akbar privately appealed to him!

Nor do I intend to dwell on the tortured political history of my beloved country. As a government employee my father remained a discreet distance from politics. That has always been my attitude, too. Unlike a few of my friends in the Pakistan team, I am simply not interested in politics. I think it is of some interest, however, to place my birth in the context of Partition.

Father reached Karachi, to report for duty in Pakistan just five days after Independence. He immediately applied for leave of absence to see his first-born, Syed Zaheer Abbas. He held me in his arms for the first time in the September. This is how he remembers it:

As I stepped into my ancestral home in Sialkot, my wife greeted me by placing the baby in my arms. He was awake, lightly dressed for the summer. His eyes were open, his fists clenched. He was roundish, plump and warm. The child filled up my arms and felt comforting. God was merciful in bestowing upon us a son healthy and bright, to reinforce our ambition to see the offspring grow into an asset of pride for the parents, for the family, and for the country which had also been born free and independent within a few weeks of Zaheer's own arrival in this world.

Two months later, my father was posted as officer-in-charge of the locust-control outpost at Turbat, in the southern section of the desert called Mekran. It was a perfect breeding ground for the migratory locust swarms from across the Gulf. The summer months were long and dry and temperatures touched 50°C (122°F). As for the people who lived there, they were hardy and robust. They lived and thrived on goats' milk and the finest dates.

My father's work took him on frequent tours of locust-survey deep into the desert.

Zaheer Abbas was therefore the darling of his mother. That, however, did not hinder the development of a chummy and intimate friendship between my son and myself. We felt all the more close and comforted when we met after intervals. In the cool of the early mornings and evenings at Turbat, we spent our time together in promenades with the baby in arms ... As if two years of privation and the aloofness of desert life were quite enough to give a tough and vigorous grounding to any small child, my department decided to recall me for duty at the headquarters in Karachi.

Here was a new luxury which my father could hardly have expected so soon. Karachi was expanding rapidly and there were population problems. But we were allocated government quarters in an area where we had space almost as big as a football pitch in front of the buildings. In the middle of the field there was an improvised cricket pitch. Small boys watched with envy

Family group from the Fifties.
Young Zaheer is standing next
to his mother.

Zaheer's mother.

and excitement. I was one of those wide-eyed spectators. It was my first sight of a game which was to provide me with a living and international recognition.

I still remember how the walls of the government quarters served as a boundary. I still remember how I longed to pick up a bat and see if I could do the same as the older boys. My father was later to write:

> Did sights like this captivate Zaheer's heart for cricket or was he born with the game in his blood? It would be difficult to say. But he lost no time in wielding a bat himself—from the moment he grew big enough to hold one. There were so many children from the government quarters that it was no problem for him to collect enough to bowl and field for him.

Apparently I was destined to be a batsman. In the memory of my father, I preferred others to do the fielding. Good friends of mine may be inclined to chuckle and imply that it is still the case.

My affection and enthusiasm for cricket probably took my family by surprise. Father was a studious man who in the mid fifties, in fact, was to attend a course at Cambridge University. He was organised and disciplined in his professional life; he was well read. And he envisaged me growing out of my boyish cricketing notions and getting down seriously to my studies. There was talk of a degree in medicine. My parents must have felt that I was devoting too much of my spare time to matches on the improvised pitch in front of the quarters.

Even before I was seven I used to take part in village matches. Sometimes I went on my bicycle. On occasions it meant crossing a river. I couldn't swim but one of the older members of the team would take me on his shoulders. We would dry out in the sun and head for the ground. It wasn't quite the kind of village cricket they play in England. The wicket was often bad and the scoring none too accurate. In my quiet, undemonstrative way, I relished every minute.

There are so many of my childhood memories still recounted regularly by my parents with affection and pride. I stand aside again for my father:

Zaheer as a young boy gained admission to a school in a village close to Sialkot city. At the end of his first academic year he completed his period in the nursery class. But at that stage he didn't know the difference between 'pass' or 'fail'. He came running home from school one day, happiness on his face. 'I have failed my examination . . . I have failed, father.' The first reaction of his mother and myself was that he had lost a valuable year in his early studies. We made our own inquiries and discovered to our pleasure and relief that he had gained good marks, in fact, and had been promoted to the next class.

My son never liked the sight of a policeman in uniform. When he saw a traffic policeman on duty, Zaheer was apt to turn his back. In 1952, Zaheer's uncle became a lieutenant in the army and one day he turned up at our house in military uniform. My son didn't approve at all. He looked at his uncle for a very long time and then, after recognising him, said: 'So you have also become a policeman!' This uncle, S. Zulfiqar Ali Kermani who later became a major (dental surgeon) had a great liking for Zaheer and in later years, as he noted my son's promise as a cricketer, promised him 100 rupees for each century scored. There were many such rewards up to the time Zaheer became a Test player.

During his school days, I recall, Zaheer once went to play a local match in the suburbs of Karachi. At the time cricket kit was very costly and his team had only two bats between them. In the course of the game one of the bats got broken—and the other also developed a bad crack. Worse, Zaheer was using it at the time. He was going well and approaching his century, but what could he do? A new Test cap, Mr Ghulam Abbas was playing for the opposing side. Zaheer was reluctant to go up to him himself but asked one of his team-mates to do so. 'Tell him both our bats are broken—and can we borrow his?' To the surprise of Zaheer and the other players on his side, the new Test man wouldn't agree. The implication was that Zaheer might play some cross-bat shots and so damage Ghulam Abbas's bat, too. Zaheer was rather upset. He murmured to his team that it was a lack of courtesy and that

77

newly-capped Test players assumed too much. 'One day I shall become a Test batsman also—and I promise I'll lend my bat in an emergency if anyone asks to borrow it!'

At family evenings at home, as I sit with my parents, we still discuss and chuckle over such incidents of long ago.

Mohammed Ali Jinnah, our first Governor-General, the Quad-i-Asam (Great Leader) was, with good fortune, a cricket lover. A domestic competition bears his name and I shall discuss it in more detail later. He and those who followed him ensured that cricket would survive the demoralising sporting effects of Partition. It has been a difficult process and we are proud of the line of richly-gifted players that Pakistan has produced.

We were admitted to the Imperial Cricket Conference by 1952, following tours by the West Indians and the MCC. There were financial and administrative problems to overcome. Until the sixties, our cricket was played on matting wickets. Very few could beat us in those conditions, although Richie Benaud managed it at Dacca in 1959–60.

Cricket remained for me something of an obsession. Perhaps I should quote my anxious father once more:

It was becoming irresistible for him and creating a problem. Cricket was a constant distraction, pulling Zaheer away from his books. I could see him developing his own style, eliciting admiration of his friends and colleagues, and compliments from his games masters at school. This offset my efforts to persuade him to cut down on his play and devote more time to studies . . .

One day he went to see me off on the train. I was going on duty and entitled to travel by air-conditioned coach. At the railway station I let him feel the cool and savour the comforts of my carriage. Then I took him around to see for himself the contrast of travelling conditions in a third class compartment. I pointed out that to live in and enjoy the comforts of life, one had to choose a career and work diligently to make it a success. Would cricket be that career for him?

I'm not sure I fully appreciated my parents' concern. The subtlety of my father's message at the railway station failed to make its impact. My devotion to cricket increased and the tour and inaugural Test matches of the Pakistan team in England in 1954 generated more excitement and enthusiasm than ever.

Gradually my father accepted that I would never be putting on a doctor's white coat. He even used to sit on a chair in front of the government quarters after office hours and watch me practising. It pleased me to see him there and I tried even harder.

Father had been an athlete in his college days. He had an appreciation of a good stroke but was never a cricketer himself. So there was no parental coaching. It has always been a claim of mine that my style is my own. I developed on my own initiative, devoid of tuition and coaching. I watched great players and sub-consciously may have been influenced by them. I tried to avoid copying anyone.

Maybe this is a good moment to talk of my heroes and the influences on my cricketing life. Hanif Mohammad was, I suppose, the first. I went to the Test matches at Karachi and watched some of the world's great players. Colin Cowdrey was to me a slow player but I marvelled at the way he placed the ball. Ted Dexter always seemed superb off the back foot. Tom Graveney—who preceded me at Gloucestershire, of course— was magnificent for his cover driving. But Rohan Kanhai was my greatest hero of all. I would sit in wonderment as he scored his runs. No-one could compete with him in my mind, though in more recent times I've seen some wonderful batting from Viv Richards. It was a great thrill for me when I found myself batting at No. 4 to Kanhai's No. 3 for the Rest of the World against the Australians in 1971–72.

Yet there came a time when my father's realistic and persuasive words had their effect. I accepted—though I was in no sense an academic—that I must put cricket temporarily to one side and obtain a university degree. In a calculated way I switched from the sciences to the arts. I had never enjoyed the practical scientific studies in the laboratories. I worked out that history would be altogether easier for graduation. I did my High School from Jehangir Road in 1964 and Intermediate Science (F.Sc) from the same college in 1967. Then I completed my

Bachelor of Arts course at Islamia College in 1969. I studied hard by my standards and for a number of years hardly picked up a bat. It was the responsibility of a son to his parents.

There was a nominal attempt by me to join the army. My heart was not in the interview. I was coming inevitably to the conclusion that I was only at my happiest when I was scoring runs.

Indeed I had already scored many. I captained my school and college and was in 1967 made captain of the Karachi Cricket Board to play in the inter-Board tournaments in Pakistan. There were many big scores for the leading local club, Park Crescent. While I was studying for my BA degree, Pakistan Works Department invited me to play for them: I decided I could do both.

Apparently impressed by my performances in the various national tournaments, Pakistan International Airlines asked me to join them. The cricket liaison with PIA has continued till the present day and I am proud of my record as captain with them. In 1970–71 I scored five centuries in six matches for PIA. That included a double century against Karachi A. Their captain was ... Intikhab Alam.

I'd long been an admirer of Inti. When I was 14 or 15 I used to go along with some of my friends to a private ground in Karachi where some of our best players would go for practice. They started at 3 p.m. We got there three hours earlier to make sure of some batting.

One day I was batting when Inti arrived early. He bowled at me—and seemed to approve of my neat, natural style. I remember him looking down the wicket at me approvingly as if to say: 'Who's this young lad in short pants?' It was the start of a lengthy and happy association.

In my school and club days I scored many hundreds. The standard of the bowling varied and so did the wickets. I remember few of the innings specifically. There was one for Park Crescent which must have had some merit because I saw my picture in the paper next day. My maiden century in first class cricket was 197 against what was East Pakistan, at the Karachi National Stadium.

There appear to be varying impressions about the standard of domestic cricket in Pakistan. I am in no doubt: it is higher than county cricket in England in many ways. Perhaps it is more relaxed but competition in the Quaid-e-Asam Trophy is undeniably keen.

The wickets are usually slow. Some of them, it must be admitted, are not particularly good. Lahore is far and away the best. Karachi is a disappointment to me and I have hardly known an important match there without crowd trouble. At times, because of that, I almost hate playing in my home city. The behaviour of the spectators can be very embarrassing. Facilities at the National Stadium are certainly bad. Often, when you are the next man in, you cannot see what is going on in front of you. The fans throw missiles and this is their joke. They do it without malice but it can be distracting and upsetting. For the players, cricket is a job—and not a joke.

Long ago I discovered, too, a reluctance on the part of the Pakistan spectator to accept defeat. He can be fickle and even turns on us if we lose.

Autograph hunters are perhaps the same around the world. Those in Pakistan are unrelentingly persistent. If you are tired and try to walk past them, they insist. As an introvert, it is a facet of cricket which I don't enjoy.

Adulation is a considerable compliment to the recipient. It is also two-edged. International sportsmen often cry out for privacy. Some of us are worse than others in handling it. I have more than once shut myself away in a hotel room. I am grateful for the warmth of public feeling towards me and proud to represent my country; but I recoil instinctively at the sight of scores of fans, waiting for a signature and expecting light-hearted banter at the end of a tiring day at the crease.

Najma estimates that 70 per cent of my fan mail comes from India. It is an interesting statistic and no doubt emanates from that very successful series I had against India in 1978 when I finished with an average of 194. They used to say I never left the crease—and monopolised the television screens!

I went back to India and was a good deal less successful. But the ardent young Indian supporters chose to remember me at my best. Friends told me of one Indian boy, probably 18 or 19, who had somehow saved enough money to watch Pakistan wherever they went on tour. 'I travel just to watch Zaheer,' he told them.

In our Bombay hotel, there were fans clamouring around everywhere in the lobby and outside, waiting for the team's return from the match. I had Najma with me. They were kissing my hands in the lobby and even in the lift. It was incredible— and overwhelming.

But I am diverting. My upbringing in Pakistan had never hinted at this kind of public acclaim. I had watched my heroes mobbed by the spectators after playing at the National Stadium but had no reason to imagine it might even happen to me one day.

Nature did not make me gregarious. I am a listener rather than a talker. I don't like parties. As I shall explain elsewhere in this book I don't really enjoy sponsorship gatherings. I am happier at home with my wife and small daughters than swopping cricket stories in a hotel lounge. I have six younger brothers and a sister, though we are not especially close. Yet I have a special regard for the intimate circle of the family; I still remember warm friendships with neighbours and chums from school and college days.

I have grown up in a deeply religious household. I learned to believe in one God, Allah, with Mohammed as his prophet. The Koran was my bible. I was taught that all men were equal in the sight of God; as such, we rejected the caste system. There are, of course, still remnants of it and some claim they can detect signs of it during our cricket matches. I can only emphasise that a game of cricket in my mind has nothing to do with politics or social disparities.

I don't eat pork and this has never brought a problem during my time in English county cricket. Strict Moslems kneel five times a day in the direction of Mecca to pray. There are varying degrees of strictness and orthodoxy among Moslems, whether or not they are cricketers. Even in my life I have seen many changes. Fewer Pakistan women live in purdah, covering their faces with their duputta (or shawl) when they venture into the street.

Above right and above: Home from England, in garlanded triumph, after the 1971 successes.

Apart from my period with my father at a desert outpost, most of my life has been in a city. I have missed the more primitive side of Pakistan existence and in many ways I have been privileged. This I acknowledge with some gratitude. I have seen the parched rural areas with their small, rectangular houses of hardened clay or mud bricks. I have seen the infertile desert and the rocky terrain—and people eking out a living without modern aid or a semblance of sophistication.

So of course I am lucky. Sialkot, where I was born, is well-known for the manufacture of sports goods. Cricket bats, tennis, squash and badminton racquets are made here; so are hand-stitched football covers. My father has a native pride about such matters. He reminds me that football covers from Sialkot were used during the 1982 World Cup in Spain.

And then there is Karachi, where I have lived, grown-up and played so much of my apprentice cricket. It's an important seaport and fronts on to the Arabian Sea. From my home I can see the ships pass by. Nowadays there is a population of well over three million. We have a modern mosque and a statue of Queen Victoria, just in case residents want to be reminded of former British rule. The streets are wide, the buildings have a look of relative affluence. There is a sporting tradition and this is the birthplace of many of our current Test players, among them Javed Miandad, Mohsin Khan, Haroon Rashid, Iqbal Qasim, Sikhander Bakht and Wasim Bari.

Lahore, second largest city to Karachi, is 800 miles away. It is famous for its mosques and mausoleums, and was a favourite centre for the Mogul emperors. Recent Test players born there number Imran Khan, Saleem Malik, Mansoor Akhtar, Mudassar Nazar, Abdul Qadir and Sarfraz Nawaz. The two cities, as it can be seen, are a great source of cricketing talent.

My present home in Karachi is three miles from the city centre, and a mile from the sea. Najma decided on the design and also, in effect, landscaped the garden. It is a four-bedroom bungalow with a large lawn and three red marble porches. There are roses in the garden and motia that smell rather like honeysuckle. I leave my wife to buy the plants and a gardener to make sure they grow. My wife has plans, she tells me, to

84

convert one of the rooms into a cricket-haven, to display the bats, the trophies and some of the records.

It would be dishonest of me to say I don't enjoy reflecting on some of my past successes. I have always been motivated by records. A double-century may go into posterity, a nought is forgotten by the next morning. Every time I walk to the wicket I hope it will be an innings to be remembered.

Pakistan, the Islamic Republic, has fashioned my personality. During my lifetime it has been restructured and re-divided. There have been tensions and bloodshed. In my history lessons I learned the awsome background of the Indian sub-continent. I listened—yes, always I listened—to passionate arguments about Moslem and Hindu, about East Pakistan (now Bangladesh) and Kashmir, on street corners and cricket pavilions.

Here, in what is now Pakistan, Rudyard Kipling lived and wrote. As a country it has a past of turmoil. Its present is burdened with some problems but it has a romance all its own. Some of our Test cricketers are criticised for being supposedly volatile. Yet they are merely reflecting the exciting, instinctive characteristics of their nation.

Zed the Cricketer, peering down his glasses and not suffering fools, has been shaped not by the whims of Lord's or a coaching manual but by centuries of Islamic history.

I was a modest scholar. I failed to wear the doctor's white coat that my father had once foreseen, or the military uniform that I almost impulsively chose. Some of my brothers are more accomplished in the professional and commercial sense. My talent, as I was first to discover as a five-year-old after wading through the river, was to hold a cricket bat with style. I went through the motions of study, acquiring a degree and placating my family at the same time. I steeled myself, against all my inclinations, not even to touch my beloved bat for several years. But it was really self-delusion.

There are precious few facilities to encourage the development of cricket talent in Pakistan. Little, in the practical sense, is done in the schools, colleges and universities. There are no publicised national coaching schemes for promising schoolboys. The young cricketer progresses solely by his own initiative.

Never once did I need anyone to fire my imagination and point me in the right direction. It seemed for me the most natural thing in the world that as a small, starry-eyed boy I should go out on the improvised pitch in front of the government living quarters in Karachi.

Cricket came naturally to me. I found I possessed rhythm, balance, timing. I was never scared of a fast bowler. Pakistan club cricket was always teeming with extravagant leg-spinners. Unlike in England, they are not an unfashionable and discouraged breed. I relished the challenge of countering a turning ball.

Would natural gifts and an insatiable appetite for the game be enough? Could there really be a living in professional cricket—as then still meagrely rewarded—for me? Was I too naive and unworldly? Did I have any inkling at all of the vast gulf between a relaxed Quaid-e-Azam fixture and a dour, often unloving Test match at Sydney or Headingley?

My parents and my brothers looked at each other. It was 1969—and I was about to find out.

The unknown Zaheer Abbas was selected to play against New Zealand at Karachi. I made an inauspicious 12 and 27. There followed an unlikely tour with PIA to Ireland, whose cricket team had, after all, recently beaten the West Indies. Ireland, I remember, was wet; but my scores were 62, 67 and 44.

Then I equalled Hanif's record by scoring five centuries in a domestic season. That helped to ensure a ticket for the Intikhab 1971 party to England. And that, in turn, made a career in English county cricket virtually inevitable.

It is a good point on which to pick up the thread.

Surrounded by his complete—and—proud—family in 1971.

Just one of the many reception committees, waiting for him on his return after that Edgbaston double-century. This large group includes the chairman of Karachi Port Trust, officials of the Karachi Cricket Association, and local journalists.

PLAYING

County Cricket—but no Cap

My decision to sample county cricket in England seemed such a logical progression if I wished to build on my early measure of success and to play the game I loved for as many months of the year as possible.

Friends of mine at home sensed my aspirations and warned me lightheartedly that I should miss my beloved chicken tikka curry and a gentle-paced, privileged way of life that were precious to me. Nor, they reminded me somewhat pointedly, was my knowledge of the English language excessive.

'I'll let my bat do the talking for me,' I joked. I have always relied on its eloquence to carry me through. Never have I been one of the world's greatest talkers. My bat relishes the opportunity to hold court and attract an admiring audience.

There were other possible careers in the offing for me in Pakistan; my father would willingly have guided me into the kind of job that carried both prestige and a sizeable salary. That was why, with paternal wisdom, he had insisted that I should concentrate on my studies and equip myself, at least theoretically, for the kind of post that was emotionally and professionally a long way removed from a cricket ground.

I had made my centuries for school and college, for my leading club side, Park Crescent, and for Pakistan International Airlines. Against East Pakistan in the Quaid-i-Azam Trophy I'd failed by just three runs to make a double century; under the eagle eye of Intikhab in 1970–71 I'd reached five centuries in six matches. My 202 had been at the expense of his Karachi A.

Apart from my Test debut in 1969 against New Zealand, a modest enough introduction for me in the personal sense, I had actually gone that year to Ireland with PIA. Abstemious as ever, we ignored the Guinness and got on with the cricket. There were plans for me to come to England in 1970 with an Under-25 side; reverberations of South African politics, prevalent at that time, ended those arrangements and I remember being very disappointed. With single-minded application I compiled as many runs as I could in domestic cricket. I feared that I might be forgotten after the New Zealand match. Runs—and that meant centuries for me—seemed the most forceful argument for ensuring a place in the touring party for England during 1971.

My head was racing ahead of me. Impressive form in the Test matches appeared to me the right kind of prelude to county cricket. I would also have the chance to talk to other Pakistan players already established in England. I'd be able to discover whether those English wickets were as green and difficult as everyone seemed to claim.

The story of my cricketing life over the next ten years or so was to prove rewarding, eventful and at times decidedly dramatic.

There were the rewards of prolific run-making, eventful episodes that ranged from Packer to Pakistan politics, and even the horrific drama of a murder on the fringe of my English county club. But more of all of that later.

I was on that 1971 tour of England, of course. It was memorable for so many reasons—I was first to reach 1,000 runs, by early June, and there was my innings of 274 in the opening Test. Zaheer or Zahir, the sub editors couldn't decide which, was all of a sudden a new name for the headlines on the sports pages. Despatches sent home to Pakistan were glowing in their praise and I was instantly popular with my dressing room colleagues. A double century overrides all as a passport for popularity. The Board at home was purring with pleasure and no-one was ready to believe that I'd had very little coaching in my cricketing apprenticeship. For me, the important factor was that I had, in one wonderful match at Edgbaston, established myself as a Test player. I recall the surging consciousness of national pride: here I was playing for my country against the best in the world. Simultaneously I was still a boy in my sporting emotions and I was thrilled with the romance and the glamour of the whole thing. I felt good.

Several English counties had begun to show an interest on the strength of my newsworthy introduction. They started 'phoning around, asking indirectly about my availability. 'Does this chap Zaheer want to have a go at county cricket? What's he like as a person? Can we tempt him?' A few of my team-mates were tapped in the politest sort of way. It was rather nice to feel I was in demand.

Sadiq Mohammad was already with Gloucestershire and I discussed the implications very thoroughly with him. Let me see, wasn't this the county of the great W. G. Grace and Walter Hammond? I'm very impressionable where names are concerned.

Grahame Parker was Gloucestershire's secretary-manager at the time. Majid's father knew him and I was assured that he was a thoroughly nice and honourable man. He and the Gloucestershire committee were also resourceful, sensing that there was competition. 'You must get Zaheer,' Sadiq was telling them with kindly enthusiasm. Mr Parker set off for Bradford where the Pakistan tourists were playing. It was raining and we met, for the first time, in the pavilion. As he remembers it: 'Mushtaq and Sadiq were also present and they all chatted away in Pakistani above my head. I felt like a kind of Tommy Docherty out to get my man! The following match was against Oxford at The Parks and I made another visit from Bristol. Again it was a wet day and we went back to the hotel. And Zed agreed to come.'

As far as I remember, my basic salary was to be £1,750. At the time, the prospect of playing county cricket, with all its fine traditions, was so much more important than financial considerations. Later in my career, an added element of professionalism and a more astute attitude to the game, influenced by my own maturity and the indirect persuasions of others, made me look more carefully at money when it came to contractual discussions.

And so it was that I arrived in Bristol in 1972. My English was still modest. I was conscious of being an object of curiosity. West Country supporters wanted to take a look at this so-called

Outside the county ground at Bristol, with the W. G. Grace tablet on the gates.

A faded and nostalgic cricket snap. Zaheer dons his arguably delayed county cap, watched by colleagues Sadiq Mohammad, Roger Knight and skipper Tony Brown. The year . . . 1975.

Zaheer looks in at the Gloucestershire headquarters after his 1982 tour matches have ended. Not much sign of spectators for this 2nd XI fixture.

emerging star of Pakistan cricket. Press and radio reporters came to interview me. I smiled and did my best but I fear that their questions were longer than my answers. I found Bristol geographically confusing; so many of the little suburban streets around the county ground looked identical to me. It seemed an unwise policy to venture too far from Nevil Road. I spent a great deal of my time in the nets—I'm never homesick in a cricketing environment. Back in my flat, despite a kindly landlady, I felt lonely and strangely isolated. This aspect of being suddenly separated from my fellow countrymen and my family had never really occurred to me. My Irish landlady, Mrs O'Brien was like a mother to me. I was able to confide and take my troubles to her.

The best antidote to loneliness, I decided, had to be *cricket*. But I knew that my first-team appearances in my opening season for Gloucestershire would have to be limited. I was eligible, all the same, for the visit of the Australians to Bristol at the end of May. My net practice was prodigious as ever (as 'Inti' is apt to say I don't ever want to leave the wicket, not even in the nets!). I was determined to make an impression on my first official match for the county. And David Colley had me caught for 12. I didn't bat again.

There were 2nd XI matches and Under-25 matches. I remember early on scoring a half century against a Warwickshire 11. Their side included Dennis Amiss and Bob Willis. I didn't realise then that the tall, fiery, rather ungainly Willis, who took three wickets in the second innings, would end up captain of England.

My personality is naturally withdrawn and introverted and I am, for instance, a good deal less outward-going than Sadiq who appeared to have no great difficulty integrating into the general banter of the county dressing room. In my case, it was much more of an effort. Tony Brown and the players encouraged me to extend my faltering English vocabulary; they often had fun, I noticed, at the expense of Sadiq. I had friends in London and whenever I had the chance I travelled to their home, up to several times a week.

My first county game was to be at Edgbaston towards the end

of July. I was already in love with that ground. I mused pleasantly at my experience there the previous year. My return was on this occasion a good deal less than ecstatic. McVicker bowled me for nine.

I had 14 championship innings in 1972 and scored 353 runs. When we got to Cheltenham in mid-August, the Gloucestershire players said to me: 'This is a ground where the spinners always have a chance.' They've been saying that, I understand, since Townsend, Dennett and Tom Goddard were curling their fingers round the ball.

Against Middlesex I felt I was getting the hang of English wickets—and Cheltenham, in particular. John Price bowled me for 75 in the first innings and Phil Edmonds got me for 58 in the second. I liked the academic atmosphere of that ground straight away. The billowing tents, the subdued voices of the clergy and the old soldiers, and the evidence on the boundary of College boys who had plainly chosen to delay their holidays . . .

Just after the Cheltenham fixture we went to Taunton. I was told this was genuine West Country rivalry, although I must say I didn't see too many signs of it. The idea of a 'derby' match at county level is more in the minds of the spectators than the players.

It was a pre-Richards Somerset. They had not yet generated the remarkable enthusiasm which has been such a feature of the late seventies and the early eighties. There was, however, more visible passion for the game than for the most part we found in Bristol. I have always been impressed by the way Somerset cricket fans get loyally—and noisily—behind their team. In that 1972 match there were whoops of delight when Hallam Moseley bowled me for a duck.

I was more introspective than usual as I flew out of London, bound for Pakistan. I had pleasant things on my mind—all of them to do with marriage.

Bristol, I had realised weeks earlier, was no place for a single man many miles from home. I was to be married in the October. And I was just about to meet my wife for the first time.

People in the Western world find it hard to understand the marriage customs of my country. I can only say that the

Arranged Marriage, with its roots firmly in religion, has a reassuring success rate. It succeeds because both partners work at it; they prepare themselves mentally and philosophically for it.

Najma, my wife, comes from Sind. Her late father was a successful businessman and landowner. He owned a flourishing cinema near their home. She had a privileged upbringing. The girls in the family had a special nanny and there were up to four families of servants. She had always lived in the Karachi area and had much socially in common with me. She did well in her studies, especially geography and English, and hankered after a career as an artist. Maybe it will be of interest to the reader to hear how she viewed the impending marriage!

Of course I'd heard of Zaheer but had never met him. I was still doing my studies when he made his marvellous 274. But I'd watched him on the telly and was thrilled with his success. I had always admired sportsmen and was very impressed with the fact that he was so famous in such a short time ...

His parents came to see me and approved. My photograph was taken and sent to Zaheer, along with the photographs of other girls. This is how it goes. The photographs were accompanied by relevant information. It was now up to him to decide, although the final word naturally rests with the girl.

Zaheer, I knew, was lonely and did not want to remain a cricketing bachelor in England. He wanted an educated girl and a sensitive girl. He wanted one who could help him with his specific problems, and assist him with his English. It was made clear to the girl that she would be marrying a sportsman who would often be away from home.

He arrived off the plane and came straight to see my family. I liked him when I looked at him. I liked his quiet disposition, his warmth and his friendliness. It was our only meeting before the wedding. It was formal and others were always present.

I have been brought up to believe in the Arranged Marriage. It is natural to be apprehensive in deciding to share your life with someone you have not met before. Everything

94

is done to ensure the perfect pairing but there must remain unknown qualities. We expect the worst as well as the best. We must overlook the less attractive side of each other. We realise that it depends on us alone—we must make it work. That is why it is so important to prepare ourselves mentally.

Just over a month after the wedding I was leaving my new bride to play a Test series in Australia and New Zealand. I should have liked to take Najma with me but it was against the Cricket Board's policy. I didn't see her again till the March; the following month I was flying back to England, my bride by my side.

Najma was confronted by a completely unfamiliar environment and way of life. The neat, claustrophobic streets of Bishopston and Horfield and St Andrews were so different from anything she'd been used to. She must have quickly missed her friends, just as I had, though she never complained. The voices and the scent of the shrubs in front gardens were strange to her; so were the groceries in the shops as she explored the busy Gloucester Road in Bristol.

I took her around with me as much as possible. At times for away matches she stayed in the team hotel. We needed as much time together as possible. Najma and I were in the process of getting to know each other. We were busy discovering each other's whims and preferences and quirks of human nature. This is the added price of the Arranged Marriage: it can also be a richly rewarding experience.

My wife became pregnant. We were enormously excited but this placed additional strains on us as we stole hours to be shared in hotel rooms and boundary seats. Najma didn't escape the problems of the pregnant wife. She was unwell at times and slightly depressed. She has always maintained that I worry incessantly when there is illness in the family. I was certainly upset when I saw her taking her pills and looking a good deal less animated than usual. She'd sit in the car, listening to the radio or reading and, for every good reason, feeling sorry for herself. I'd walk along to the car and sit with her every half hour or so during some matches, when I wasn't needed on the field.

Najma is a highly intelligent woman. Friends had helpfully indoctrinated her with the responsibilities she would be taking on as a travelling cricketer's new wife. It must still have been a frightening revelation. Remember, we'd had no more than a token hour or so to discuss the implications before the wedding.

Before she came to England she had never worked. She was still more or less fresh from college with all the advantages of a relatively privileged background opening out for her. There were others around to do the housework, the sewing and the cooking. In England, apart from the especial demands of building a new relationship to last for life, she was the cook and the housewife. She would joke to friends: 'And I hate cooking!' She also claimed with some validity: 'The trouble with Zaheer is that he wants never less than two curried meals a day. On my own, I'm happy to make do here with English food for convenience. He gets plenty of that in county cricket and he can't wait to get home for his curries . . .'

I was quite anxious about my wife's condition and, despite her comforting presence, was still having some difficulty acclimatising myself of necessity to an English lifestyle. It was apt to show in my cricket, though I spent as much time as I could at the nets. I was going to demonstrate to Grahame Parker, skipper Tony Brown and one or two mildly sceptical players and committee members that my double century in 1971 was anything but a fluke.

Initially, there were not so many friends in England. I tended to withdraw from large groups of people. I still struggled too much with the language and it simply wasn't in my nature to be gregarious. 'You'll have to judge me as a cricketer rather than a mixer,' I smiled to those who approached me.

Tom Hennessy was one of those who befriended me in the early days. He was a good-natured ex-sailor who kept an inn, the quaintly named Robin Hood's Retreat and was the personal friend of many of the Gloucestershire players. It wasn't a question of going into his pub for a drink; he and his wife, Edna, would invite the players into their private rooms and treat them as members of the family. Perhaps Tom had better explain for himself:

Sadiq, I remember, first brought Zed along to the Robin Hood, which after all is only half a mile from the county ground. Zed didn't speak very much at all. He looked to me rather lost and clearly shy. His manners were impeccable and he was a delightful chap. But he left others to do the talking. It was just hello and goodbye from Zed. I like to think I gave him helpful advice in the early days—about things like property and cars.

Our first *faux pas* was when he walked into the back room and I offered him some ham. Put it down to naivety on my part. But he used often to eat with the family at the Robin Hood. Sad and he would rush down from the county ground during the lunch hour. They used to pick up chicken and chips from across the road and bring it into the back room. Zed was very appreciative of the feeling of being part of a family, even if it wasn't exactly a formal sit-down meal.

This was open house for all the Gloucestershire cricketers. I was on the committee at the time and they knew my great affection for the game. None of the players had much money in those days. Many of them used to share digs. They certainly didn't have any money left over for booze, whatever one or two of the committee used to think when personal form was suffering a bit! Sad and Zed weren't interested in the drinking, anyway. They'd sit in the armchair, watching the television as they ate their chicken and chips. They'd call Edna 'Mum' and there was a touching little scene on Mothers Day. They turned up very self-consciously at the back door with some flowers. It was very comical and moving at the same time.

Soon after Najma arrived in Bristol, Zed came to the Robin Hood. She remained outside in the car. I sensed that she probably didn't approve, although she was assured that Zed only called in when he was feeling lonely for a 'tonic' or two.

'Go on, Zed, bring her in.'

'I don't think she will come.'

Najma was persuaded. She was a tall, beautiful woman, warm and friendly. Trying to be hospitable I poured her a dry, white wine. With a courteous smile, she left it. But it was the breakthrough. Soon Zed was inviting Edna and myself out to sample one of Najma's curries. It was a tricky moment—I just don't like curries. With a succession of tactful excuses, I still haven't taken up that particular kind invitation.

In every way, Zed is a gentleman. I remember the first time I met him was the day before my daughter Christina's wedding. There was a reception at the Anchor Hotel and a number of the county players were asked. Zed came, a quiet, pleasant, slightly bewildered guest.

I used to pick him up in my car from Temple Meads station when he arrived in April from Karachi. In an odd way, I felt Gloucestershire should have put out the red carpet for him. He was, after all, an exceptional cricketer, a great world class player. Instead, I recall a chilly April with snow on the ground—and here he was straight from sunny Pakistan. He'd write to me five or six weeks previously. 'I want my White Daddy to find me some digs.'

One rather sad memory of Zaheer remains with me. I'd gone to Temple Meads as usual and the train was already in. There he was, alone on an otherwise deserted platform, surrounded by his cases and other luggage. He was a long way from home—and there had been no-one to meet him. He looked lost and unhappy.

My 1973 season for Gloucestershire brought me 780 championship runs from 30 innings, two first class centuries and a final average of 30.

It started with great promise. I went to the Oval in May and scored 153 not out. The *Bristol Evening Post* got excited—and so did some of the county committee. On the circuit, Gloucestershire were being complimented on their opportunism in signing me. 'Wait till we get him on a few green wickets,' said a few of the canny seamers.

I suppose it was a fair point. I had to wait till the end of August before I reached another 100. It was against Somerset at Bristol, I was sent in first with Sadiq and Brian Close bowled me for 103. In that match I sensed his considerable presence in the

Somerset side, whom he had joined to the dismay of some loyal Yorkshiremen. It seemed to me that Yorkshire still needed him but that county's judgments were as eccentric to me then as they are now. Closey bowled me with not one of the better deliveries of the day; nor was it one of my more memorable strokes.

There were some cheap dismissals—and lessons to be learned. I was inclined to take my worries home with me and my new wife had no need to ask whether I had made a good score. The climate was not often conducive to the compiling of runs for a Pakistan stranger; I shivered in two sweaters, I waited impatiently for the rain to stop. And I discovered that the docility of the Oval wicket in early-season was deceptive. Trevor Jesty was getting some movement off the pitch to bowl me for a duck almost immediately afterwards. At Worcester, in July, a bowler called Brian Brain was seaming the ball very cleverly indeed to get me for three. We played Worcestershire for a second time a month later at Cheltenham, I remember, and the young Imran Khan complemented his studies at Worcester Royal Grammar School by dismissing me twice. He'd played in one of the Tests against England in 1971 and could hardly have imagined that eleven years later he'd be captaining his country.

Back in Bristol, Gloucester and Cheltenham, I sensed muted enthusiasm about my ability to adapt to English conditions. Not for a moment did I share such apprehensions, whatever the bizarre behaviour of one or two tracks. The 1973 season of championship cricket was perhaps not quite one to cherish. But there were one or two modest landmarks. At Old Trafford, my delicate off-spinners were officially recognised. I took my first championship wicket. My victim was Farokh Engineer. And maybe there is more than a hint of irony in the fact that he was born in Bombay.

There was plenty of time during that summer, as I waited padded-up or was alone in my hotel room at night, to take stock of my new county. It was a period of transition. Formidable figures had just left or were on the point of doing so. I'm thinking of Arthur Milton, David Allen and Ron Nicholls, Barrie Meyer (who could have guessed he would become such a respected umpire?) and John Mortimore. And David Green, of the rugby player's muscular build and eloquent bat, was leaving cricket earlier than expected for a career in the catering industry, now in turn passed over for a seat in the press box.

'Morty' was a quiet man, a thinker. I quickly discovered he had a clever and dry sense of humour. He was studying hard for accountancy and players joked that John was the best chap to work out your expenses.

The atmosphere of the dressing room must have changed. There were now three overseas players. In addition to Sadiq and myself, Mike Procter was winning sweeping admiration everywhere for his all-round skills. In those more agile days of mine, I fielded at slip to 'Procky' and gazed in awe of him as he pounded up to the wicket off that long, fearsome run. He wasn't quite in the Lillee and Thomson bracket, or that of Mike Holding, fastest of them all in my assessment, but he was very pacey indeed and there wasn't too much around on the county scene in England to compare with him at his breeziest. As a batsman he was tremendously entertaining and a stylist too, and the two don't always go together. I'll have more to say about his dynamic hitting.

As a foreigner I have a sharp ear for dialect. I quickly warmed to the Devon voices in the Gloucestershire team. There was Jack Davey, with his cheerful Tavistock manner even when his bowling was being hit. And, of course, David Shepherd, son of a North Devon postmistress. If he had a weight problem, it went with his good-natured demeanour. Crowds loved him, not just because he was slightly ungainly but because he hit the ball very hard. He ran singles as well as anyone in the side. His late-evening claims that he was once a sprightly scrum-half may well have had foundation. He was a good influence in any dressing room.

Many of the stories about Gloucestershire cricket over the past twenty years, for instance, feature 'Shep'. All are told with affection.

Back in the Swansea team hotel one evening during an away match with Glamorgan, 'Shep' seemed in the mood for a practical joke. He picked up the local telephone directory and chose a name and number at random. When a colleague (not a tale for names to be repeated) came in, he was told by Shep that a girl called Jane had called and left her number.

This caused both embarrassment and some consternation. 'Jane, you say ... Who-who's Jane?'

'She didn't give any details. But, well, you know, it must have been that one from a couple of years ago. Remember?'

The sinned-against member of the Gloucestershire team innocently 'phoned. By one of those odd coincidences there was a daughter in the household called Jane. But the father had answered the 'phone. For several minutes there was a strange, evasive conversation. The father was not in the best of humour and he probably didn't like cricket.

The young cricketer, renowned for both a sense of fun and a modest reputation as a philanderer, looked back across the lounge. He caught the grins on the faces of his team-mates. Faster than it normally took him to take guard, he made his excuses and left the 'phone.

Offsetting the more carefree side of first class cricket in England, I detected the tensions and the personal ambitions.

Roger Knight clearly had leadership qualities and he fervently hoped his travels would end with Test recognition. His medium-paced bowling was never quite penetrative enough to make him an outstanding all-rounder but he could bat with tenacity and enthusiasm. David Graveney and Julian Shackleton were young players who knew they were saddled with the formidable reputations of other members of the family. Andy Brassington, a highly promising wicket keeper from the Midlands, probably agonised—despite that lovely, bouncy exterior—that he couldn't bat just a little better. Harold Jarman asked for only enough senior matches to demonstrate that he could make runs with the same facility as he scored a record number of goals as a winger at Bristol Rovers. The cricket scope never quite came, though he ended up briefly as a third division soccer manager as some kind of compensation for someone who loved the summer game most passionately of all.

Gloucestershire won the Gillette Cup final in that 1973 season and I shall refer to that soon. Some of the young players always seemed to me just a little too self-effacing. Modesty is an

Who would dare to have reservations about Zaheer's fielding on this evidence? Against Hampshire at Bristol in September 1977, he snatches a fine slip catch to dismiss Barry Richards. The bowler is David Graveney. Stumper Andy Stovold and Alastair Hignell watch admiringly.

endearing quality but professional sport calls for burning self-confidence, too. I may not succeed every time I walk to the wicket but I invariably believe that I am going to. I was interested to hear the Barbadian all-rounder John Shepherd say, soon after joining Gloucestershire from Kent, that they looked like a side unused to success. It wasn't meant as a criticism; but at Kent, he'd experienced regular title-chasing. And there was a different attitude of mind in Bristol.

Rarely in all the time I have been with the county have any young players come to me for technical advice. The coach, of course, is the proper counsellor, although I know from personal experience it can be of great help occasionally to have a confiding word with a senior player.

My 1974 season with Gloucestershire was severely limited because of Test match commitments. I played in only four county matches but at least got some valuable early batting practice with a century at Fenners against Cambridge University. I have few Bristol memories—apart from the murder.

Simon Kerr was a twenty-year-old Rhodesian who showed considerable promise as both a cricket and rugby player. In search of wider experience of first class cricket, largely on the recommendation of Mike Procter, he became a short-term employee of Gloucestershire CC. It was intended for him to play 2nd XI matches and help the groundstaff. He was a quiet, popular young man around the county headquarters, after arriving in the May of 1973. By the following March he was dead, brutally murdered in a basement flat not far from the county ground. The cruellest aspect of all was that he was a completely innocent victim.

Simon had been invited to a Saturday night party and was put to bed in the basement after having rather too much to drink. At about 3 a.m. he was stabbed by Desmond Carroll, a fellow guest whom he didn't even know. A kitchen knife with an eight-inch blade was used and left in the chest. In evidence, Carroll said that the idea of stabbing attracted him. He was jailed for life by Mr Justice Park.

It was Tom Hennessy again who worked tirelessly with great compassion to soothe the distraught and distant Kerr family in

Rhodesia. He wrote them copious letters and talked to them on the phone. He campaigned for the body to be sent back to the family as quickly as possible for Mr Hennessy, my White Daddy, had numerous letters of gratitude from Simon's parents.

County colleague Jim Foat was at the same party. But the whole club was grieved, not least Procter, who held out such hopes that young Simon would follow him as an established member of the first team.

His sudden death shocked and saddened the Gloucestershire team. I had come to know Simon quite well, liked the look of him in the nets and found him easygoing and good-natured. He would have been good company at any party and the last person to be associated with any unpleasant incident. I read the details of his death in the local papers and found it hard to accept the truth. All the players felt a great surge of sympathy for Simon's family.

I return understandably with haste to the cricket. My county cap was awarded to me in 1975 and, in honesty, I had hoped that on my reputation as a Test player, it would have arrived earlier. I wasn't around much the previous summer and Gloucestershire wanted to be sure, I suppose, that I was good enough. The county cap, I was told, wasn't handed out to players who could make 200 against England; they had to prove they could do it at Swansea, Chesterfield or Folkestone.

My county batting average in 1975 shot up from 29.57 to 47.53. I scored 1,426 runs, which was twice as many as I had compiled in a previous season for the county. There were centuries at Cheltenham and Trent Bridge; against Nottinghamshire, I failed by eight runs to make it a 100 in each innings. I also remember my fleeting annoyance when John Snow got me caught for 98 at Eastbourne.

There was just the suggestion of a smile on my face when Intikhab dimissed me cheaply in Bristol and our eyes fleetingly met. I should have known all his leg-break and googlie wiles by now from shared days with PIA. We always enjoyed our encounters when on opposite county sides. Two years earlier at the Oval, I was not the only century-maker. Intikhab and Sadiq both reached three figures ... Talk about Pakistan dominance!

Some of the county bowlers in England were beginning to feel they knew my vulnerability. Boyce had me twice at Westcliffe, Dye twice for Northants. When it came to Worcester, it was Brain again. He came later to Gloucestershire and I thought wryly to myself that it was just as well to have him on my side.

I did some serious analysis when I next flew back to London. My wife and I felt a good deal more settled. My daughter was a constant source of pleasure to me. I now had my own home in Bristol and although I was far from the best gardener in the road—almost a non-existent one, I fear—I had persuaded a good friend from the county groundstaff to keep the lawn in trim.

Harvest Time

Sunshine greeted me in 1976. It was the hottest summer for years. The fields were parched and the reservoirs were nearly dry. But the wickets were full of runs. It was time for me to capitalise, time for me to make my mark on county cricket. I knew there were still some who believed I was incapable of emulating my best Test match form at county level.

For most of the season I headed the national batting averages. I reached 2,000 first class runs on 9 August, the earliest since 1965. I scored eleven centuries; against Surrey at the Oval and Kent at Canterbury, I scored a double and single century without ever being out. Maybe by now showing off a little, I rounded off the season with a century before lunch at Worcester. My aggregate for the season was 2,554 (av. 75.11), the best since Bill Alley's 3,019 in 1961.

I do hope this isn't starting to sound like a boring catalogue of personal achievement. It's important for me to pause at this stage of my career in English cricket. This was the year when, for all sorts of reasons, I proved myself. At home, my family were joyfully pasting my records into a scrapbook. Someone at the county ground was heard to say: 'Good job we didn't leave it another twelve months before giving Zed his cap.' Sadiq was joking: 'Pakistan is where all the good players come from.'

Soon it was the turn of *Wisden* to say complimentary things. At the end of July, 1977, Sussex came to Cheltenham. The College trace was less charitable than usual to the spinners; the batsmen came out on top and 1,143 runs were scored. 'I'm glad to say that after all that, Gloucestershire won by eight wickets.

Everything else in this match was dwarfed by the batting of Zaheer, who set a world record when he became the first player to score a double and a single century for the third time. Remarkably, his other two performances, against Kent and Surrey in 1976, finished not out like those in this game.

For his 205 in the first innings he did not offer a chance, although he lofted the ball more than usual.

World records are very much my target. They fire and motivate me. Every time I walk to the crease I push myself statistically. I hear other players say that records mean nothing to them. They mean a great deal to me and it would be dishonest to overlook the point.

I relished every innings at Cheltenham that season. Someone worked out that my average there was 216.

Then I packed my bags and motored off to Southampton. I was dreaming of runs and couldn't wait to reach the wicket. And I scored my third successive century, 100 not out. That meant I'd clocked up 413 runs in those three innings and I hadn't been dismissed. As I made my nightly 'phone call home to Najma in Bristol, the lilt in my voice told it all.

Maybe it's time to bring myself abruptly down to earth once more. The 1976 and 1977 seasons overflowed with runs, assurance and good strokes from me. But when the West Indians came to Bristol in '76, Mike Holding had me caught for a duck. The Australians arrived there in '77 and again I failed my team and the supporters. Max Walker took my wicket—for 0 and 5.

I've cause to remember especially two of my half dozen centuries in 1978. They followed each other at the end of May.

We began by going down the motorway to Taunton, ran into trouble against Ian Botham and were forced to follow on 237 runs behind. Ian kept firing bouncers at me. He'd apparently been warned about sending down too many of them in the previous match but that didn't deter him. I made 140 out of 198 in just over three hours in the second innings but it wasn't enough to save us from defeat by ten wickets. It should be recorded that Botham stuck to his guns and his theories about short-pitched deliveries—and got me with one on the final morning.

Then Gloucestershire went off to Hove. We seemed to be making a habit of trailing badly on first innings. We batted first and made 129; Sussex with a complete lack of mercy—particularly by century-maker Imran—replied with 424. That didn't leave us much chance.

Our skipper Mike Procter turned to me when it was my turn to bat a second time: 'It's up to you, Zed. Stay there and make a game of it.'

I managed to do that. I stayed to score 213—and Sussex finished a truly thrilling match at 84–8, vainly trying to get the runs. They failed . . . by two.

There were, of course, the benefit matches. I'm not sure how much the average player enjoys them, however relaxed and lighthearted they may appear. Most professional cricketers are tired from an exhausting schedule of county matches, one-day and three-day. That involves some bizarre cross-country journeys and at times the minimum of sleep.

But there are the benefit games and we turn out for our team-mates in afternoon and evening fixtures when we are expected to flex our muscles and heave as many sixes as possible. The end result for the beneficiary varies markedly. One bonus for the players is an education tour of the West Country. We all have our endless stories to tell. Here is just one from Tom Hennessy:

It was Proc's benefit and we were spending a few days in Devon. The team had played one match at Paignton and now had to find their way to a hotel at Exmouth. There were rather a lot of stops and then the rallying call from official Frank Twisleton: 'Come on, lads, let's get the show on the road.' We set off in strict convoy but not for long. Of all things, I found myself following those two utterly reliable West Countrymen, Sadiq and Zaheer. We ended up rather near Barnstaple in North Devon, as far as I could gather! But at least Zed and Sad were resplendent in their new denim suits they'd bought from a Pakistan dealer they'd met at the game.

Perhaps I should be grateful that I wasn't in the Gloucestershire side that played at Basingstoke in a testimonial match. There was a champagne party in one of the tents and the players were invited to go along to a benefit darts match held in one of the large pubs in the area.

The Gloucestershire players set off from the team hotel in five cars. There were three in David Shepherd's car and he imperiously led the way. The much-told version of what happened next was this: 'Suddenly Shep had to brake. Tony Brown's car went into Shep's car and damaged the bumper. Tom Hennessy collided with the rear of the skipper's vehicle. And so it went on. Proc went into Tom and Roy Swetman, bringing up the rear, completed the multiple collision.'

There have been slight variations in the re-telling but it was substantially true. And there was nothing worse than thick heads when play started next morning.

A book like this must be an honest record of the subject's thoughts. I must say that I have never been quite at ease with some of the peripheral activities of county cricket. The organising of a benefit year can be, as I now know from personal experience, a matter of some anxiety. Players' relationships with the sponsors can also be a delicate matter.

I was criticised in a recent book by Brian Brain, *Another Day, Another Match* about my attitude to the sponsors during a short period in 1980 when he was in charge of the team. He wrote: 'One thing only marred my time in Folkestone. I had to report Zaheer to Tony Brown and Procter for refusing to attend a function in one of the sponsors' tents. I didn't want to do it but I felt he'd undermined my authority by refusing to come with us.' He went on to say that he didn't know how he would have handled the situation if others had followed my lead . . . 'When I told Procter and Brown about the incident, they said I had acted correctly. I have no idea what disciplinary action was subsequently taken.'

Let me try and explain my point of view. I hope that it reflects in no way a lack of courtesy to the sponsors. Their financial assistance to the game, at national and county level, is enormous. I was sorry that Brian Brain, a player with whom I got on well, should have chosen to air publicly this small incident. We played together numerous times afterwards, following the book's publication, and my attitude at Folkestone that evening in 1980 was not discussed again.

I am paid to play cricket for Gloucestershire—to perform for them on the field and help them to win matches. My contract is for the scoring of runs.

Am I being naive or unreasonable in arguing that I am not at a game of cricket to do a promotions job for the county *off* the field, too?

That evening at Folkestone I had made arrangements to go off with Asif. My job of work as a cricketer had been completed for the day and I now wanted to relax with a friend. If my absense from the sponsors' tent upset anyone I am sorry. I cannot believe that it was even noticed.

At Cheltenham I dutifully went to sponsorship events a large number of times. The attitude of many non-cricketing people present perplexed me. I do hope it doesn't sound arrogant to say that the cricketers often walked around unrecognised. I remember occasions when guests in the tents didn't even know Mike Procter. It made me think at times: whatever is the point?

As the game of cricket becomes even more dependent on the generosity of sponsors, it is possible that the players will be expected to play an even more visible public relations role. It isn't something that all of them naturally enjoy. They may not be socialisers or relish carrying on polite conversation after a perspiring day in the field. They are grateful to the sponsors but for all kinds of physical and psychological reasons they like, in many cases, to get away from the ground as quickly as possible.

All professional cricketers have their prejudices. Mine don't include participating in one-day matches. I can accept their appeal to the crowd, although I'm full of sympathy for those players who are forced to slog from the moment they reach the crease. It is often against their natural style and they risk ridiculing themselves, as professionals, in front of spectators who are more intent on fire than finesse.

Over recent years I have taken part in various single and double-wicket challenge matches. They usually carry a tempting financial inducement and it would be hypocritical of me to imply a lack of enthusiasm for them. The chemistry never quite worked in my match against Viv Richards at the county ground in Bristol, sponsored by the local car firm, Bryan Brothers. Don't ask me why. I look on Viv as a dear friend of mine and have unstinting regard for his peerless batting. Some in the crowd that day maintained that the attitudes of Viv and myself at the wicket varied too much—that Viv was carefree and there was not too much evidence that his heart was in the result. On the other hand, I was supposed to be deadly serious and intent on winning. Certainly in some ways the match lacked a competitive edge and it caused the sponsors to switch to double-wicket the following year.

This time the Gloucestershire-Somerset rivalry was deliberately intensified. It was Mike Procter and myself against Richards and Botham. Intikhab took a therapeutic break from managing the Pakistan tourists to join the guest bowlers and remind us all how well he could still turn the ball. Somerset, alas, won; now for the excuses. Proc had flown over from South Africa and probably lacked batting practice. He'd have been prepared to have a match or two for the county as he was still registered as a player. David Graveney as the captain no doubt had difficulty deciding how he could suddenly accommodate the former skipper on a short-term basis. So Mike patently needed match practice. I was also in poor nick and there'd been hardly any batting at all for me since I'd gone off to join the tourists in preparation for the first Test of the 1982 season. It was not Gloucestershire at its best.

I got the clear impression that the real drama of the day happened off the field. Lunchtime was fast approaching when the sponsors discovered to their horror that through some administrative slip-up at the Taunton end, Viv and Ian didn't even know the game was on. They had it pencilled into their diaries for the original date, later in the month. A 'phone call to the Somerset headquarters caused panic stations all round. The help of the cricket committee chairman, Roy Kerslake, was enlisted and with a mixture of desperate initiative and good luck the two great players were located and dispatched hot-foot to

Bristol. The first over was not due to be bowled till late afternoon and the Somerset contingent made it with half an hour or so to spare. Few of the spectators were any the wiser. In the interests of discretion, nothing was said about the absent VIPs at the sponsors' special lunch.

And more drama up in that lofty and rather precarious press box. An imposter, claiming that he was the official representative of the *Daily Mail*, was escorted out by club officials and police officers. His audacious resourcefulness, it emerged, had over previous weeks been causing some concern to the club.

There will doubtless be more challenge matches and more cricketing experiments in the pursuit of money-making and entertainment.

I was due to take part in an inaugural floodlit cricket match at Ashton Gate, home of Bristol City Football Club. The square leg boundary didn't seem much more than the distance between the wickets. It poured with rain and umpire Bill Alley, in sou'wester, traded jokes with the bedraggled and curious crowd. Alan Gibson wrote a highly caustic piece in *The Times* and left before the end.

I was down to play for Gloucestershire and there was some surprise when I failed to make an appearance. 'Is Zed showing his contempt for this kind of cricket?' they asked.

The truth is that I turned up and had every intention of playing. But as I wear glasses, it would have been quite impossible to bat in that kind of weather.

My goodness, I've digressed long enough. I must return to 1979—and with it my memories of a drawn game at Taunton in the August. It was a marvellous match and I'm told it ranks with the very best clashes ever between the two West Country sides.

The first day was lost completely to rain. There followed, in the true spirit of cricket, three declarations and so nearly a result. Both sides declared on 200 in the first innings. In the process, Procter offered a quite incredible exhibition of hitting. Poor Dennis Breakwell, tossing up his left-arm slows on a length, was savaged. Over two overs, Proc hit him for half a dozen successive sixes. Most of them were just golfer's chip shots—it all looked so ludicrously easy. The secretary's old wooden hut out in the car park was battered with missiles from out of the sky. Others landed in the churchyard. When Proc put one six through the open window of the players' viewing room, Brian Brain at last came gingerly into focus waving an improvised white flag.

And so it went on, though not so dynamically. In their second innings, Somerset scored 263 for two. Brian Rose and Phil Slocombe both hit centuries. The mood of the match had by now pulled in more supporters than you usually find for a championship fixture towards the end of the season. We were left to get 264 and ended at 246–8. With eleven overs to spare we were only 39 short and had five wickets standing.

My own contribution was perhaps not in the Procter mode. But I like to think it was alert and adventurous. I scored 147 out of 210 in 146 minutes. Proc took 25 minutes over a half century and had been in 46 minutes when he was out for 93. I hit nine sixes and eleven fours. And I was out when 28 runs were needed from the last four overs.

All the players enjoyed the match, even Dennis Breakwell. The memories, I've discovered, go back a long way at Taunton. 'Sammy Woods, Guy Earle, Harold Gimblett and Arthur Wellard would have been proud of that kind of hitting—and that's a compliment,' they were saying to us afterwards.

'Biased blighters!' someone from our dressing room said. 'What's wrong with Gilbert Jessop?'

I must say I always enjoyed playing in Somerset. In 1978, '79, '80 and '81 I reached centuries, three times at Taunton and once at Bath. That made me, I was politely told, a troublesome adversary. Maybe it was as well I couldn't interpret some of the rustic vowels. The remarks would, I'm sure, have been good-natured.

During the 1980 fixture, Botham—by this time beginning to assume the appropriate nickname of 'Beefy'—flung his bat marvellously for 228 in 184 minutes. He set up a record fourth wicket stand for the county, I remember, with 'Dasher' Denning, who just stood there in awe, as his partner tried to put the ball over the church tower.

Alastair Hignell (100 not out) and myself (173) scored 254 in three and a half hours. We saved the game and I was in danger of being called a slogger by my wife!

As a county, Gloucestershire could be exciting and infuriating. We lacked consistency. In 1976 and 1977 we were third in the championship. There were encouraging innings by Andy Stovold. Chris Broad was soon to come through as a left-hand opening bat. John Childs was tossing up the ball well enough surely to be near England consideration. And Phil Bainbridge seemed the most promising of all. I should like to see him play for his country and I think he will. It didn't surprise me when he was nominated as the Commercial Union's Under-23 Batsman of the Year in 1981.

That 1981 summer was a rewarding one for me. It brought me ten championship centuries, 2306 runs and an average of 88.69. I was the first to the 1,000 runs (30 June) and the first to 2,000 runs (17 August). At Bath, in mid June, I scored 215 and 150 without being out. As I'm apt to say, I'm either very good or very bad. My good seasons—1976 and 1981—are very good. My bad times, as my face and demeanour usually betray, are very bad. I was missed once at Bath but I rarely felt as though anything would get past the bat or go to hand. Somerset drew that match, as I recall, on the strength of some gritty, rearguard batting from Brian Rose and Peter Roebuck, both of whom were limping badly from earlier injuries and had hoped they wouldn't be needed.

And so to 1982 with its bitter-sweet memories. I arrived back in Bristol without Najma, daughter Rudaba, by now eight, or baby Roshana. I missed meals and ate all the wrong food. I was examined by the club doctor and given medication. I was even too weak to walk to the nets and I simply couldn't be considered for some of the early matches.

Najma's return was the tonic I needed. The day before her return I scored a century in each innings against Lancashire at Gloucester. There weren't many spectators around to see it and I heard murmurs that the future of county cricket in the city was in jeopardy.

It was also a match of severe thunderstorms and two unduly painstaking centuries by Graeme Fowler and David Lloyd, who also shared an Accrington background, so the record books told

Another effortless boundary . . . and this one is not through the covers.

(Photograph *Patrick Eagar*)

me. I was beginning to feel stronger and to put on weight again. My thoughts were on curries at home again, a renewed companionship with Najma and cradling my daughters. I was feeling happier than I had done for weeks and it was reflected in my batting.

My 92nd and 93rd centuries in the same match put me level with my Gloucestershire predecessor Wally Hammond in the world records; I had now overtaken C. B. Fry and Jack Hobbs.

Gloucestershire have had two triumphs in the one-day cricket and I mustn't ignore it. As any player will tell you, the technique is vastly different. We learn to improvise with our shots, deliberately taking advantage of the fact that there isn't a slip. If we aren't careful, we can fall into bad and untidy habits when we return to the purer forms of cricket.

'That wasn't like you, Zed,' a supporter at Cheltenham or Bristol will occasionally say to me on a Sunday afternoon, after I've made a few untypical attacking strokes.

I give them one of my wry, silent grins. They suspect, I'm sure, that I slog with an apologetic air.

In the late seventies, Mike Procter came up to me. 'How about going in at No. 1, Zed? Think about it.' I reasoned that it made sense for one-day matches; by the time I went to the wicket at No. 3, 20 overs and half the innings might be over.

It is possible to build an innings, even on a Sunday afternoon. Up to 1981 I'd scored five centuries in the John Player League (and claimed Glenn Turner's wicket with the most subtle of off-breaks, genuine PIA vintage, circa late sixties).

The Gillette competition, eventually to make way for the NatWest equivalent, had also brought me three centuries. I failed in the final against Sussex in 1973. But Proc and Tony Brown were quite magnificent, and we won by 40 runs.

It was an ordeal for some of the less experienced players, both in this final and the Benson and Hedges Lord's appearance four years later. I remember Jim Foat after a few drinks, saying: 'Zed, we've won ... we've *won*!'

I pray that I didn't sound blasé. But, by the time of the Benson and Hedges match, I'd been playing international cricket at the very top level in the tautest of atmospheres for a rather long time. Lord's was just another good match. 'Yes, Foaty. We've won.' I hope it didn't show.

The Gillette final was a great event for Gloucestershire. The players arrived on Friday night after a busy and tiring match at Old Trafford. Tactics were discussed over dinner in the hotel. In the dressing room next morning there were good-luck telegrams everywhere. I sensed what it meant to them.

Then in 1977 it was the turn of Kent to be beaten. The margin was 64 runs and it was a surprisingly good win against such one-day specialists. It was a terrific match for Andy Stovold, who went on to collar the gold award. He made 71 and took three catches behind the wicket, just to prove that a stumper is not overlooked by the adjudicator. I made 70. Kent badly mismanaged their game. They had the stronger all-round side and the more impressive line-up of bowlers. Yet none of them pegged away with the deadly economy of Procter and Brain.

Two appearances at Lord's in the seventies, both victorious, were timely boosts to Gloucestershire who had waited from W. G. Grace's days for the fillip of a title.

They are very much part of the story of my career in county cricket. But now it is time to talk also of Test matches.

I hope in this book that I've conveyed my warm regards for my county club. At the same time I must be honest enough to express a minor reservation. It was the way I was treated over my reasonable wish to wear a floppy hat

This is the kind of headwear I invariably use in Pakistan. It's particularly suitable for me, because I wear spectacles. More important that that, I feel comfortable in a floppy hat. So it seemed the most natural thing in the world for me to want to wear one back in England, early in 1982. Tony Brown, our secretary-manager at the time—he has since moved to Somerset—was clearly not in favour.

I was just about to take the field in one match when he implied that floppy hats were definitely out as far as Gloucestershire were concerned. I honestly thought Tony was joking. But when I discovered he was serious, I was rather shocked. Where hats are concerned, I feel an experienced cricketer should be able to make up his own mind.

The idea was that our county players would all look alike, I suppose. I didn't make a fuss and left my floppy hat in my cricket bag. Yet it appeared to me an odd and unnecessary rule and, inwardly, I was just a little resentful that despite my loyalty and successes for Gloucestershire, I was being very firmly forbidden from wearing the kind of hat that was now, in any case, becoming a familiar sight in championship matches.

*

'Testing' Times—and Triumphs

My Test debut was made against New Zealand at Karachi on 24 October 1969. That date will never elude my memory—and nor will my two innings of 12 and 27. The kindly, encouraging Intikhab was my captain and I batted at No. 5. He detected the self-reprimand on my face when I gave needless catches, first to Murray and then Burgess. But it was, all the same, quite a demanding baptism to international cricket. From early on the first day the ball was chipping away fragments from the wicket and it remained responsive, if not all-embracing at times, to the spinners.

I was twenty-two, at once excited and apprehensive. My family and friends were there to watch me. I had both a boyish sporting fervour and a sense of national pride, I remember. At home, before I went to the ground, I stood in front of the mirror, bat in hand.

Runs were never going to be easy for anyone. Pakistan took nearly six and a half hours, circumspect in those capricious conditions, in making 208 runs. I admired Sadiq that day. He scored 69 and stayed for four hours. No-one was going to shift him; I realised then what a bonny little fighter he could be.

He was one of three brothers in our side. There were also Hanif and Mushtaq Mohammad. When I eventually got to Bristol, where the boundary historians are infallible guides to such family distinctions, I was assured that a trinity of Graces, W. G., E. M. and G. F. played against Australia in 1880. Similarly three Hearnes played in the same Test in 1892; in their case, Alec and George played for England, and Frank for South Africa.

The idea in those days was for pitches to be prepared to encourage a positive result in four days. It was fine for the bowlers but it provided an unsatisfactory imbalance and the art of batsmanship suffered. I should perhaps not have been too disappointed with my modest Karachi aggregate.

In 1970–71 the Pakistan Board introduced a new BCCP Trophy to take the place of the Ayub Trophy. The records seem to show that it was very much to my liking. I had a particularly fruitful season and my intimate friends said they could see me visibly growing in confidence. Playing for Pakistan International Airlines, I scored 962 runs and that gave me an average of just over 100. The season brought me five centuries— and four of them came in consecutive innings. It made me immensely happy. My philosophy towards cricket has never remotely changed; when I am scoring runs I am at peace with the world. There is sheer joy in my disposition.

In the March of 1971, playing against Karachi Blues in the final of the competition, I made 202 not out. It was my first double century and I knew there would be others. That is meant to reflect a single-minded will to succeed and amass large scores and does not, I hope, hint at any kind of personal conceit.

I really believed I was heading for a century in each innings in that memorable match. PIA declared their second innings when I was 81 not out.

I was conscious that I had suddenly matured as a batsman. With a minimum of coaching, I had managed to absorb and reproduce many of the skills I had seen in my heroes. Those I imitated were the cricketers who hit with a straight bat and viewed batting as an art form. An ugly shot has always made me wince. Cricket to me is the most beautiful of all games—and there is infinite beauty in a cover-drive or square-cut.

That row of centuries was, of course, marvellous for my morale. My father nodded with approval. Public acclaim was a new experience; oddly, it was something I savoured best of all in retrospect and in the privacy of my home. We are all made differently. It isn't in my nature to wave a bat at the supporters. My appreciation is none the less genuine.

Like all batsmen I have had lapses of inconsistency. In that

1970–71 season, however, the runs were multiplying and my smile of satisfaction was broadening. In 45 innings up to my selection for the England tour of 1971 I had scored nine centuries. I had willed myself to be in that tour party. Statistics, I felt, were the best argument of all.

After an apparent eternity of suspense I discovered that I had been selected. I didn't jump in the air; my emotions are usually kept well out of sight. But those close to me knew the extent of my pleasure. Family friends converged with congratulations. I mused to myself on the words of my father to his landlady when years before he was studying in England: 'I don't know if I shall be back—but my son will be one day.'

I packed my bags and boarded the jet. I spoke not too many words in English but such prosaic notions weren't even in my head. I was off to play cricket for my country . . . in *England*.

The opening tour match, in the tradition of the time, was at Worcester. It struck me as a handsome ground, with its fine cathedral not so many boundary lengths away, chiming out during the match. The weather was ideal, leading me to wonder why everyone had forewarned me about a supposed amalgam of wind and rain.

If this was one of those so-called green wickets, I told myself, then I had absolutely nothing to fear. It was a lovely track for batting and Glenn Turner stylishly exploited it. He made 179 and his county declared at 305 for five. That left us 25 minutes before the close and we lost two wickets. Not so good.

My first innings on English soil was to prove memorable, all the same. I made 110 in two hours 25 minutes. The outfield was fast and I was able to penetrate the off-side fielders regularly with shots off both the front and back foot. It was the perfect debut and earned me the headlines—even if I had a little trouble with the translations of the various reports.

The cricket writers sent back equally glowing accounts to the papers at home. These were painstakingly cut out and pasted by the family into a scrapbook.

Every time I have returned to Worcester, whether with Gloucestershire or the Tourists, I have fondly remembered my arrival in 1971. My most recent visit was with Pakistan in the

July of 1982. Again the sun shone and I listened to the chimes from over mid-wicket. The atmosphere is tranquil, just like this intimate city itself. I have no especial favourite ground in England but Worcester holds for me the glow of warm memories.

I waited three weeks in 1971 and scored another century. This time we were at Gravesend where the pundits seemed to imply that there wouldn't be any play at all. It was a reasonable conclusion; on the previous day the pitch was under water.

This was to be my first look at Derek Underwood, whose reputation had of course preceded him. 'He's unplayable after the rain,' everyone was saying. 'There's no-one better in the world in these conditions.' The record book was inclined to bear that out. I was still young to the game, my mind uncluttered by prejudices, fears and forebodings. My mental attitude was right, my confidence was high and I had no tiresome hang-ups about technical flaws. Pakistan batted first and made 299. My share was 138.

I was enjoying myself in England. I failed by just three runs to score another century, at Trent Bridge this time. During May my total was 731 runs and I was determined to establish myself fully by the first Test on 3 June.

As a touring side we came painfully unstuck at Fenners. Pakistan had lost their first three wickets for five runs. I went in at No. 5 and was top score with 47. Asif (45) and myself were the only players to make runs. In the second innings I followed up with 62 but Cambridge went on to win their first match against a touring side since they beat New Zealand in 1927. I'm not sure what my father, also a Cambridge man, made of that . . .

The Edgbaston Test. Ah, yes, a mighty landmark for me. Here I became a man and my dreams were fulfilled. Here was the sheer pinnacle of my aspirations. Here, in Birmingham in 1971, I confirmed those rash, romantic prophecies I made to my father. However long I go on playing and however big the innings, I shall not surpass the elation and psychological achievement of that Edgbaston.

It was my personal statement.

Perhaps I shall be forgiven if I once more unashamedly parade my enthusiasm and joy. It was shared at the time by my nation. Cricket historians and friends at home still quote it.

When the Pakistan team arrived at the ground I was 261 runs short of my 1,000 for the season. By 4 June, the second day of the Test, the target had been passed. I discovered it was the fastest 1,000 runs in England for a dozen years and they were scored, as one august publication pointed out with generous observations, at 'a quicker rate than Bradman.' I mention it as a statement of fact. You will find no fatuous comparisons in this book. How pointless such an exercise is; my style is a mile removed from that of the magnificent Bradman.

I scored 274 in that Test match. It was the highest by any batsman appearing in his maiden innings against England. It was also the first double century by a Pakistan player against England. My second-wicket stand with Mushtaq was a record for my country. In that match I know I blossomed as a batsman. I felt utterly in control. As I passed 50, I aimed for 100; then 150 and then 200. And then 250. I wanted never to be out. I was hungry for more and more runs; I was greedy, too, if you like. I was playing for my country, for myself and for the record books. As each four through the covers earned applause from a good-natured crowd, I was only impatient for the next half-volley. My whole approach to cricket was encapsulated in that innings.

When Brian Luckhurst caught me off Ray Illingworth, I was momentarily cross with myself. I adjusted my glasses self-consciously, ran my sleeve over a perspiring forehead and through mingled emotions I half-heard the collective response of the crowd. The England players were clapping me and murmuring 'Well done' with genuine, if wry, smiles as I walked back to the pavilion. I was something of a hero as I was welcomed back by my team-mates. I flopped on a seat, grateful for the acclaim. I knew that I had arrived as an international cricketer.

I didn't have a chance to bat in the second innings—and not much chance in the next Test, at Lord's. Seventeen hours of play were lost to rain. We only had time for one innings and I was top score with 40.

123

Peter Lever got me that day and I was soon facing him again when we went to play Lancashire. His seam bowling provided all sorts of problems and needed the greatest attention. We made 195 for nine declared and I took some personal satisfaction from scoring an undefeated 100. It sustained my confidence for the approaching third Test match, at Leeds.

This was my first look at Headingley, a venue familiar enough to me from Test match commentaries that I had listened intently to as a boy. Lever was again my downfall but not before I had scored 72 and was again the most successful Pakistan batsman. I draw a discreet veil over my second innings; the Luckhurst–Illingworth combination accounted for me before I had scored.

That was the end of the series. I had played in every match of the tour and my aggregate was 1,508, with an average of 55.85. My ego was enhanced when *Wisden* observed: 'The discovery of the tour was undoubtedly Zaheer.'

I had plenty of time to ruminate on the 'plane journey home. My captain, Intikhab Alam, had constantly encouraged me. He had warmed to my strokes and enthused about my form; there was, he assured me, a long Test future ahead. There were all sorts of compliments flying about from scores of Pakistan well-wishers in England and I knew that there would be much delight when I returned to Karachi.

It would be dishonest to imply that I didn't relish the compliments. I was going home to what I suppose they call a hero's welcome. Rather grandiose claims were being made about me. Here, the papers claimed, was the emerging new star of Pakistan cricket. My double century had brought me instant fame but I imagine I remained rather unlikely material for a glamorous figure. I was as quiet and introspective as ever. The English cricket writers called me 'studious-looking'; maybe that pleased my father.

On that 'plane home I relived almost every shot I made in my innings of 274. I confess it with the hope that it doesn't make me appear too self-centred or obsessed with my own performances. Rather, I like to think it illustrates the way that batting dominates, even takes over, my life. If someone, a stranger, asks me my occupation, I'm tempted to say that I'm a batsman just as someone else will reply that he is an accountant or civil servant.

'Of course, we should have won that first Test—that was the tragedy,' we all agreed.

We had every reason to curse the English weather. Throughout the match we held the initiative. We made England follow-on and would certainly have won but for rain on the final day. Pakistan had felt very pleased with their 608 for seven, even more so when England were dismissed for 353. At the end England were 184 for three and we sensed victory. Play didn't start till after 5 p.m. on the final day and then came bad light.

Yet there were five centuries and my double century was only four runs short of Denis Compton's 278, England's highest against Pakistan, at Trent Bridge in 1954. I batted for nine hours ten minutes and hit 38 boundaries before being out to the sweep. I quote now from *Wisden*:

> Zaheer and Mushtaq Mohammad enjoyed a record second wicket stand of 291, while Asif with 104 emphasised Pakistan's immense batting strength. England would have been in a sorry state but for Knott's attacking 116 in the first innings and Luckhurst's defiant 108 in the second.
>
> Pakistan must have been surprised at the ease with which runs came after winning the toss. Ward's third delivery struck Aftab Gul on the head and he had to retire to have a wound stitched. This brought in Zaheer and one soon appreciated that he was a batsman out of the ordinary. He was particularly strong on the leg-side, piercing the field with ease. Sadiq's was the only wicket England took on the first day when Pakistan finished 270 for one (Zaheer 159, Mushtaq 72). The pair scored 82 in an hour after tea. Next morning, Mushtaq was out after batting nine minutes short of six hours (for 100).
>
> When he reached 261, Zaheer became the first batsman to complete 1,000 runs in the English season. He said afterwards that he had not felt too tired and was thinking in terms of a world Test record just before he was dismissed.

Wisden perceptively made the point that in those days I made many of my runs on the leg-side. That is perhaps hard to believe; it is as a result of playing county cricket that I have strengthened my off-side repertoire. Now everyone tells me that my best shots are those through the covers. Maybe they always *look* the best but the art of batsmanship encompasses shots and deflections on both sides of the wicket.

In an article for *Cricketer International* in 1976, all about Test match double centuries, Irving Rosenwater saw the achievement as one of temperament as well as skill. He listed some of those who failed ever to reach 200 in a Test: they included Grace, Fry, Ranjitsinhji, Cowdrey, Sutcliffe, Woolley, Hassett, MacLaren, Woodfull and Macartney.

> In the whole history of cricket only two men have ever scored a double century on their debut. R. E. Foster against Australia, 287 in 1903, and L. G. Rowe against New Zealand at Kingston, 214 and 100 not out in 1971–72. Zaheer Abbas and David Lloyd scored a double century in their second Test (Lloyd 214 not out against India at Edgbaston in 1974). It took Don Bradman and Len Hutton six Tests to become double centurians.

In an editorial for *Playfair Cricket Monthly*, Gordon Ross asked what constituted a great player and what was the clear line of demarcation between a good and a great player. This is part of what he had to say, just a few weeks after my Edgbaston appearance:

> Perhaps the one word that tells all is *class*: a high pedigree of quality and, most of all, authority. Peter May was a great player ... it was utter domination over bowlers and an unrelenting determination to prize his wicket highly and never give it away. Bradman had the same rare qualities: his psychological approach was even more rigid than May's. How then do we begin to look at Zaheer Abbas, the young man from Pakistan. One man, another truly great player, watched the innings and must have put the clock back 17 years, for in 1954 Denis Compton scored 278 at Trent Bridge. Compton then, of course, was a mature player, the

great improvisor who, because of his immense skill, could throw orthodoxy to the four winds. But however stern we are in trying to analyse Zaheer's performance in terms of a beautiful wicket and only moderate English bowling, it is still an innings which must qualify him for the list of possible great players in the making. Time alone will tell whether he has the skill and temperament to touch the top. His past record confirms that he might have.

Have Pakistan produced another Hanif, but with more flowing strokes than Hanif? What course is Zaheer's cricketing future likely to take? Has he been approached by more than one English county already; if so, will the amount of cricket played over here blunt his edge? Whatever happens, apart from making Pakistan cricket history, Zaheer has ensured the success of the tour.

With every justification, Mr Ross posed a lot of questions. He had every right to wonder aloud whether Zaheer Abbas, at the age of 23 and still a newcomer to the ways of cricket at the very top level, would build on that double century. I chuckle as I read, at this distance, his speculative reference to a future for me in county cricket.

It may appear immodest of me to reprint an article which vaguely puts me in the bracket of great players. I am simply trying to convey the volume of interest and crystal-gazing generated by that single innings of mine in Birmingham.

At no time was I in danger of getting above myself. There were always wise, experienced men within my own dressing room to keep my life in perspective. And Ray Illingworth was in no mood to allow me the bonus of reassuring ideas. He wrote generously enough, immediately after Edgbaston: 'Zaheer is a great timer of the ball and his talent is undeniable. But I do not see him as a bogey man in the other two Tests. I think he could be vulnerable on pitches with more life and bounce in them.' A sting, indeed, in the tail although I think I have a reasonable case for contesting his words.

In his book *The Cricket Revolution*, Bob Willis described my English Test debut as 'an amazing performance, even though it was on a typically docile Edgbaston wicket.' Unlike *Wisden*, Bob was more impressed by my off-side play.

> But he also lashed into Derek Underwood, smashing him through the on-side. In fact, Underwood was dropped in favour of Norman Gifford after that Test. Only the West Indians and Kim Hughes in Australia have played Underwood as impressively as Zaheer in all my time in the England side.

Willis always seemed, nevertheless, to have some reservations about my ability to bat when the ball was moving sharply off the seam. In some of my early games for Gloucestershire, I accept that I was in trouble. The Willis verdict was this: 'He remains vulnerable to the moving ball. He plays high pace extremely well off the back foot, using the speed of the ball to play his shots in the mode of Glenn Turner. Highly talented, he plays beautifully on the off-side; a very wristy batsman, he is adept at playing down the ball on the rise. I would always back a high class seamer like Chris Old or Mike Hendrick to trouble him in England, even though he is a big innings man on flat Test wickets.'

My Test career continued in Australia the following year. Neither there nor in New Zealand, immediately afterwards, did I excel. After two failures at Adelaide, I felt I was going well at Melbourne. And so I was; but human error intervened. I was run out for 51 and 25. There were sympathetic words for me on my return. Such sentiments mean nothing in the record book. I went on to Sydney and made 47 in the second innings. Dennis Lillee, whose sheer speed never bothered me, was still my undoing as he had been during my Australia Test debut at Adelaide.

In the March we moved on to play our three Tests in New Zealand. For two of them I found myself opening with Sadiq. In five innings, my highest score was 15. Who would dare to say that cricket is not the greatest of all levellers in the human condition?

There was no time for dejection or self-analysis. The next month we had a short home series against England. At

Hyderabad, at least I made my first appearance as a Test match bowler. My gentle off-spinners were well on a length and my accuracy was deftly sustained for one over. I gave away just one run; I also made a modest 24 before being caught by Roope off Pocock. With little scope in the following Test at Karachi, I began to look forward to the 1974 England series. Cricket for Pakistan, after my heady arrival, was in danger of becoming something of an anticlimax and I was determined to avoid that.

I found no instant remedy when it came to Headingley in July. The runs were starting to mount when Hendrick, a bowler I never under-estimated, had me for 48. Alan Knott caught me in both innings; then at Lord's, Underwood twice took my wicket when I had scored a single run. It was a wretched match. The rain came down, the covers leaked and I never had the chance to get going.

Tour matches had gone well, however. We'd got to the first Test without a defeat in nine fixtures. Seven of those matches had been won and I got a century, I remember, against Minor Counties. I soon followed with another against Glamorgan but the thoughts of Edgbaston three years earlier still buzzed in my head and I desperately wanted success again at Test match level. It now troubled me that in a dozen matches for my country since my double century I had scored only 410 runs in Tests.

The Oval pitch in late August was slow and amiable. We declared our first innings at 600 for eight. My share was 240. But there was never going to be the remotest chance of a result. England replied with 545; Dennis Amiss scored 183 and Keith Fletcher 122. John Woodcock rather pointedly wrote of it all as 'a series that dozed off.'

I accept that in many ways the match held no more than academic interest. The bowlers had no real chance. The pitch was painfully slow and some of the cricket was decidedly dull. But I stroked 22 boundaries on the way to my 200 and like to think that whatever the overall atmosphere of this soporific match I batted with some style.

As a professional cricketer, my job is to play as well and attractively as I can—whether the pitch is sluggish or fiery, whether the conditions are humid or bracing, whether the ball is

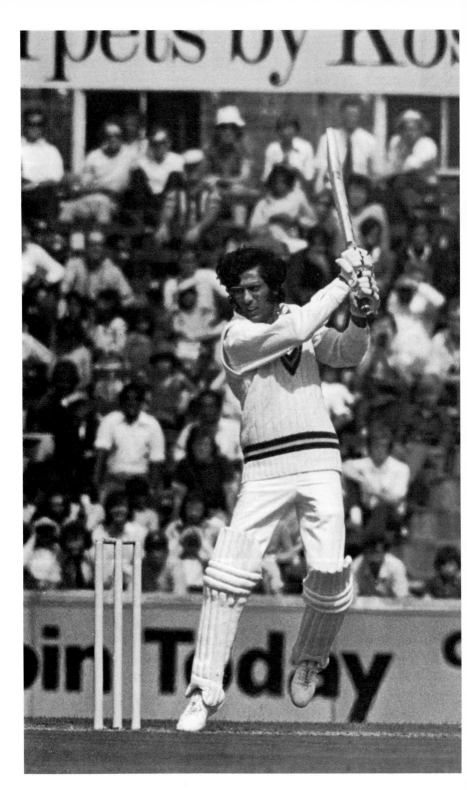

Above: Claustrophobic acclaim from fellow countrymen during that 1974 double century at the Oval.

(Photograph *Patrick Eagar*)

Right: Zaheer, up on his toes for a typical square-cut. He's on his way to that 240 in the third Test against England at the Oval in 1974.

(Photograph *Patrick Eagar*)

swinging or seaming. If it gives no semblance of assistance to the bowlers, as at the Oval in that 1974 Test, that is a bonus for me and something I must eagerly accept. I did just that. It remains, whatever the circumstances, my second highest Test score and one of which I am proud.

Straight from the Oval I went off and scored another 100, against Sussex. Suddenly I was feeling full of runs and wished I was confronted with another succession of Test matches.

Everyone agreed that Intikhab was a sound and intelligent captain. I should perhaps relate a story he likes to tell about me in that 1974 series.

> Zaheer wasn't going very well at one stage. There was a lot of pressure on him and even suggestions that he should be dropped. I could see from his face that he was worried. I went up to him one day and had a quiet word. 'You are a great player. Don't forget that. And no-one wants to drop you, not even in my case if you get ten noughts in a row. So just get that out of your system.' The last fixture before the Oval Test was at Old Trafford and he was out for 18 in the first innings. In the second innings he was going well in the forties when he suddenly signalled that he wanted to change his bat. I knew instinctively there was nothing wrong with that bat. Our twelfth man was sent out all the same with another bat and Zaheer made some vague remark about having trouble with the grip. He was out for 50 and as he came in I didn't say a word. But that evening I approached him and asked: 'Why did you change your bat, Zaheer?' He looked at me, smiled and said it was because he wanted to save it for the Test—he couldn't risk breaking it! And, of course, that particular bat brought him a double century.

It's a true story. I have a sentimental attachment to a particular bat. That one at Old Trafford felt good and I knew it would not let me down at the Oval.

All three Tests were drawn in that 1974 season and we gained the distinction of being the first visiting tour side since Don Bradman's Australians in 1948 of going through the whole touring itinerary without a defeat. It is true, of course, that we played 17 compared with the Australians' 31; on the journey home we still indulged in a little self-congratulations. Ours was a team achievement of some note, I like to think.

Intikhab led Pakistan for the two-match series at home to the West Indies in 1975 and he made way for Mushtaq when we entertained New Zealand for three matches in the October of 1976. I'd returned from a marvellous summer in England, where the sun shone continually on my back and the runs kept coming. Not so against the New Zealanders, for a second time in my case. Top score in hometown Karachi ... a rather shamefaced 16.

The Day I Broke My Glasses

Two months later, however, I was in the party for Australia. I was coming up to my 21st Test. Cricket was already a matter of playing all round the year. Friends were apt to say my eyes occasionally showed the strain; my relaxation came from the time, limited though it was, I had with Najma my wife, and baby Rudaba. Elusive family moments like that become blissful and precious to me.

Failure against New Zealand was a serious, inexplicable blow to me after the harvest of runs in England. 'I'm going off to Adelaide to make some runs again,' I promised my relatives as I waved goodbye.

It was not a hollow promise. Kerry O'Keeffe, the former Somerset leg-spinner had me caught in the first innings of the opening Test, at Adelaide, but not before I had scored 85. Dennis Lillee dismissed me in the second—when I had scored 101. It was my first century against the Australians; so it was for my good friend Asif.

Gary Gilmore bowled me for 90 in the second Test at Melbourne. One of my abiding memories of Gilmore was of a catch I took off him at Sydney. Some have mischievously implied that I am not quite the best fielder in the business. 'Inti' jokes about it at times and I admit that in more recent years I have had a tendency to withdraw from the slips to the distant pastures of third man. But in the match at Sydney, Gilmore was going well when he cut powerfully. I was fielding in the gully and as the ball flew towards me I instinctively swooped. I held the ball just off the ground and knew that it was a pretty spectacular catch and, by my standards, probably brilliant!

In my fall I broke my glasses. I have the same spectacles today and the scars of that Sydney tumble are still visible. In confidential moments I show it to cricketing friends who good-naturedly doubt my agility in the field.

We actually won the final Test, at Sydney, though I stumbled to only 5 and 4. Lillee had me both times. Our victory stilled the noisy Aussie crowd; it was our first win in Australia and only the second time we'd ever beaten them.

The Pakistan players seemed always to be in and out of jets, if not team coaches. Our next destination was the Caribbean. The West Indies battery of fast bowlers were at their most fearsome at Georgetown, Port of Spain and Kingston. Mike Holding always seemed to be the fastest of them all. God gave me a sharp cricketer's eye (forget the glasses) and an intuitive sense of timing. They are invaluable allies when the Windies are in full cry.

Test number 27 was for me a notable one. It had political as well as statistical significance. The match with India at Faisalabad, formerly known as Lyallpur, was the first between our two countries since 1961. This is not the kind of book to probe the reasons for this. The division between us is the concern of the historians and the politicians. It is at times evident in the behaviour of the spectators. But from my experience the relationship of the players from the two countries off the field is in no way antagonistic. The contact is polite and formal; if there are players with strong feelings and prejudices they keep them discreetly to themselves.

Our renewed series with India was a stirring one for me. I think Pakistan were subconsciously trying just that fraction harder. We wanted passionately to win the series and did. We started as we meant to go on, with 503 for eight; I made 176 and 96. So near a century in each innings, a matter both of regret and self-rebuke. The Pakistan total and my own contribution were records against India.

Both were to be quickly superseded. In the second Test at Lahore, our total was 539 for six and I made 235 not out. The match brought a decisive result in Pakistan's favour, an event in itself. We had to go back to 1952 for the previous occasion there

VICTORY—AND A PUBLIC HOLIDAY

It was the second Test against India, at Lahore in 1978. Pakistan won, the first time they had done so against India since 1952. As a result, the Pakistan government declared a public holiday. Zaheer's contribution was considerable. Out of a total of 539 for six, he scored 235 not out. Here are three highlights from that match. He acknowledges the cheers as he reaches his first hundred (*top, opposite page*); he is congratulated by Bishen Bedi when he gets to 200 (*bottom, opposite page*); he walks in triumph from the wicket, undefeated on 235 (*below*).

(Photograph *Patrick Eagar*)

was even a result between us. The Pakistan Government declared a public holiday. We had reason to rejoice.

In every sense it had been a good match for me. *Wisden* was especially kind: 'The extent of Zaheer's mastery can be gauged from the fact that of the 395 runs Pakistan accumulated during his six and a half hours at the wicket, his five partners mustered only 148. Mushtaq alone (67) scored more than 35. The Indians could find no way of containing Zaheer on a good wicket. The ease and fluency with which he drove, cut and pulled—he hit two sixes and 29 fours—put Pakistan well ahead of the clock and enabled Mushtaq to declare with an awesome lead of 340 runs.'

In the three Tests—and five innings—against India I scored 583 runs and ended rather proudly with an average of 194.33. My morale was high.

My sixth Test century was soon on the way, when we played the New Zealanders at Auckland in the February of 1979. If I have reason to remember this match, so surely has our wicket keeper Wasim Bari. This splendid stumper dismissed seven of the first eight batsmen—and that simply had to be a record for a Test innings.

In honesty I cannot claim that my 135 was one of my best centuries. I was actually missed off Hadlee the very first ball. I should certainly have been stumped off the unlucky slow left-arm bowler Boock when I was 90; and three runs later another straightforward catch was dropped.

I've no difficulty nominating the finest bowling performance of Sarfraz Nawaz—and nor will any of my team-mates who shared my admiration of the way he dominated the Test match at Melbourne in 1979.

He's engaging, excitable, controversial and very much his own man. He has often been in the headlines and I've no doubt he has upset a few people on the way. Pundits are in the habit of forecasting that his Test career is over; he likes proving them wrong. As a fast medium-bowler, he has the skill to move the ball through the air and off the seam.

In Australia's second innings he was magnificent. Even the Aussies grudgingly admitted it. His final figures were 9–86, beating the previous best bowling analysis by a Pakistan player

(Fazal Mahood's 7–42 almost 27 years earlier.)

The Melbourne track was getting a good deal of movement, something I found out to my cost when Rodney Hogg bowled me twice. But Sarfraz still had the stage all to himself. It was a devastating exhibition of accurate and pacey bowling and he had the Australian scribes looking up the yellowing pages of their record books for a similar deed. The best they could find for a Test match, also at Melbourne, was Arthur Mailey's 9–121 in 1920–21. He was actually the only other Test bowler ever to take nine wickets in Australia. And Mailey, so my elders tell me, was a leg-break and googlie bowler who could draw cartoons almost as well as he could turn the ball. What a marvellous character he must have been.

For the next series, starting in the December of that same year away to India, my form was disappointing and I was eventually dropped for the sixth Test at Calcutta. It was the first time, since my double hundred in 1971 that I was left out.

A year earlier there was joy and public holidays. Runs flowed from my bat and the Indian bowlers made hardly any impact at all on me. I was convinced I would simply carry on with the effortless process of making runs. It was a vow of professional self-confidence and not conceit.

Wisden was now calling me the side's 'most notable failure.' Kapel Dev was five times the cause of my melancholy downfall. India won the third Test at Bombay by 131 runs and the fifth at Madras by ten wickets. Celebrations back in Lahore suddenly seemed embarrassingly long ago. Asif had been skipper for the ill-fated series and the Board hastily replaced him by the younger Javed Miandad, whose appointed occasioned some surprise.

No-one questioned his considerable batting ability. He had scored a beautiful 163 in his first Test, against New Zealand at Lahore in 1976–77; in the same series, in his home city of Karachi, he's scored 206. But he wasn't yet 23 and was about to lead us out against those wily Aussies and then the almost intimidating West Indians later in the year.

Something I failed to avoid when the West Indians came to Karachi was a rising ball from Colin Croft. He dug it in short and it reared up to strike me on the forehead. Mostly, against the fastest bowlers in the world, I have managed by sharp reflexes to keep my head well out of danger. My batting has never been inhibited by fear.

If there was to be any fear in the following match, an inaugural Test for Multan, it had to be on the part of the spectators. They ended up, it appeared, a good deal more vulnerable than the Pakistan batsmen as they fended off the West Indian bouncers.

You will remember the game. Sylvester Clarke became exasperated by being pelted with oranges when fielding near the boundary. His form of retaliation was drastic and potentially lethal. He angrily pulled up a brick and threw it into the crowd where it unfortunately hit and badly injured a spectator. There were all sorts of repercussions and apologies. The most immediate one appeared to be that of Alvin Kallicharran who went up to the boundary rails himself and attempted to defuse the explosive situation with soothing, contrite words advocating restraint and forgiveness.

Towards the end of 1981 it was time to fly again to Australia. Oh dear, me! I have written enough already about my personally ill-fated series. I was injured—my ribs and my pride. Time will heal my more acrid memories. Not that I was exactly a failure at the wicket. I played in two Tests, scoring 80 at Brisbane and 90 at Melbourne. There was cricket to be savoured, not least Greg Chappell's beautiful double century, his fourth in international cricket. As I held on gratefully to the eventual catch, I realised just how well Gregg had fought his way back to Test form despite plenty of pessimistic predictions about his future at this level. I'd prefer to draw a veil over the rest of the series—I hope you will understand.

The Sri Lankans then arrived for a three-match series. Deep-rooted differences still existed and it wasn't until the final fixture at Lahore that four of the so-called rebels returned to the side. Maybe we felt we had a thing or two to prove. At any rate, Imran became the first Pakistan bowler to take 14 wickets in a match and going past 150 Test wickets in the process. I scored 134 and the innings took me, in turn, past 3,000 runs for my country.

We won the match by an innings and 102 runs. Mercifully, relationships were on their way back to normal. I found myself smiling again. The record books told me I'd so far played 80 Test innings and had an average of 40.85.

Frantic packing of suit cases. Domestic matters to sort out. Family goodbyes. And I was off again, this time returning to England without my wife and daughters. But the family wedding in Pakistan was postponed and Najma, an anxious and considerate wife, was soon filling my Westbury-on-Trym home once more with the comforting aroma of my favourite curries. All was well with the world again.

I was fit enough for just seven county matches before the Pakistan tour in England started. There was time for three centuries, two of them in the game with Lancashire. I scored 811 first class runs and ended up top of the county averages on 67.58. Phil Bainbridge came next on 42. 76. You can imagine I was rather pained by the speculation about the regularity of my Gloucestershire appearances in 1983.

No doubt Sadiq and Barry Duddleston, third and fourth in the averages, also viewed the future with some gloom. My Pakistan colleague, victim of the overseas rule, was selected for only 15 games and still had a useful season. He desperately wanted to score 1,000 runs all the same—and failed by two. His Gloucestershire career was virtually over and I hope his 1982 benefit, which he organised with such energy, will be a compensation. As for Duddleston, he came from Leicestershire two years earlier to help with the coaching. The county appeared to realise his value still as a player all too late. He ended up ironically with a century and what amounted to, for cruel, ecomonic reasons, the sack.

I met up with my Pakistan team-mates and they noticed that I had lost weight. I didn't bat against Middlesex, didn't play against Sussex and Glamorgan. But I made a century at the expense of a Worcestershire side of suspect strength (why are Tourists so often faced unreasonably by county oppositions of 2nd XI personnel?) and another century, this time before lunch, at Chesterfield.

That old crooked spire—I'd always seemed to play against

141

Derbyshire either at Ilkeston or Derby before—looked down on me like an amiable lucky mascot. I felt all my elusive strength coming back that day. My undefeated 148 took me 130 minutes and this was my 95th century. Now, I told myself as I came off the field, I could start counting off the remaining hundreds on one hand!

Chesterfield provided my best batting practice of an often barren season. I was particularly uncharitable, I remember, to a Malta-born, Scottish educated slow left-arm bowler called Dallas Gordon Moir. Immediately after lunch I took it into my head to go after him. I hit 32 runs in his first two overs, including a couple of sixes to prove that the interval hadn't broken my concentration. Mudassar Nazar, my partner for most of the time, was scoring his third century in six innings and was building up a temporary batting average of astronomical proportions.

It looked like a reassuring way to flex our muscles for the first Test at Edgbaston which was coming up in the next few days.

So much for successful dress rehearsals. My highest score in the three Tests was 75 at Lord's. The *Daily Telegraph* commented after the final match: 'He ended a disappointing series with an average in the twenties. What would Pakistan have given for just one of his huge scores this summer?'

Maybe I can pause and momentarily dwell on the exciting series. It produced slightly unlikely heroes like Mudassar Nazar and Mohsin Khan. It demonstrated what an exhilarating and aggressive skipper Imran could be. It gave England her first defeat against us since the days of Kardar and Fazal Mahmood at the Oval nearly 30 years earlier. It showed again how inadequately England could cope with Abdul Quadir's bewitching leg-spinners.

First there was Edgbaston. I made 40 in the first innings and remember, as I listened to the TV highlights, how the commentators remarked that I wasn't looking fit. Friends also noticed how enthusiastic I was in my applause for Mansoor Akhtar (58), my partner, as he made his way back to the pavilion. They also noted the way I had a quiet word with Wasim Raja who had called me for an unnecessary suicidal single!

But it was Lord's, high temple of English cricket, where we savoured the conquest of the host country.

Whatever the frailness of my constitution and the lethargy which I coudn't shake off, I still had my uses in that historic win. I made 75 in the first innings before being bowled by Robin Jackman. Moshin and I scored 153 for the fourth wicket, equalling Pakistan's record, set up in 1961–62 by Javed Burki and Mushtaq Mohammad. Moshin, tall and orthodox, was once dropped at slip but went on to make a memorable and almost untroubled 200. My consolation was to pass 30,000 first class runs.

Mudassar's introduction to the attack and his extraordinarily impressive figures of 6–32 are still being talked about. Inspired captaincy? Latent talent suddenly paraded? Luck? Perhaps a little of all. It's part of the absorbing, unpredictable canvas of cricket.

Pakistan won by ten wickets. Mohsin was the Man of the Match. England retired with blushes and sheepish self-analysis. David Gower was left contemplating the dubious joy of captaining his country. The Pakistan dressing room was buzzing with collective congratulations—and I forgot my mystery ailments and the bottles of tablets prescribed by my doctor.

And then it came to Headingley, where the balance swayed each day, the umpires perplexed us on an equal basis and I failed twice. England won by three wickets—and most of the Pakistan players thought it should have gone the other way.

It was quite a series. There was bad, impetuous batting from both sides: thrilling batting, too, and some beguiling bowling. We so nearly took the series. The competitive edge was always there and I'd have liked to be a spectator.

But Zaheer ... oh no! I glumly studied the averages and discovered I was a meagre 26.20. I flew home, privately pledging that I'd put on weight, somehow regain my energy and begin making runs again. It wasn't a vain pledge. We outplayed the Australians and won all three Tests. My average as 89.66.

The Aussies took a battering. Kim Hughes as the captain was on the receiving end of a fearful amount of criticism. During the

Batting during the victorious second Test against England, at Lord's in 1982.

Lahore Test, the team were accused of being 'gutless' and needed a timely statement from their manager Colin Egar to lift their morale. Jeff Thomson reverted to soccer by kicking over the stumps in the same match, after being no-balled rather too many times for his liking. Professional cricketers have come to take these kind of tantrums in their stride. It's the spectators and the reporters who choose to perpetuate the petulance.

We knew how frustrated Thomson was feeling. He'd already been out first ball. Now here he was being persistently penalised for no-balls which he apparently didn't think he was bowling. I watched the way he refused to take his cap from Shakoor Rana, the umpire, at the end of one over. That led to a few pointed words from the umpire to the Aussies' skipper, Hughes.

So . . . another relatively eventful set of international matches. And yes, there was more crowd trouble at Karachi. As I've said, there almost always is. Stones and debris were thrown in the direction of the Australian fielders. Kim Hughes twice took his players off the field and 45 minutes were lost. Barbed wire fencing was torn down. In vain, officials appealed over the public address system for order. There was even a baton charge by the police.

Forgive me if I quickly return to the cricket. We won that Test by nine wickets. Haroon Rashid (82) and I (91) were our side's top scorers. When it came to the second Test at Faisalabad, we were positively chasing the records against what we were discovering was a nondescript opposition. We scored 501–6 in the first innings; Monsoor and I got centuries. Our partnership for the fourth wicket was a record (155) for Pakistan in a game with Australia. And I became the first Pakistani to hit 1,000 Test runs against them. Najma was saying with relief in her voice: 'You're fit and more yourself again now, Zaheer. I was very worried about you.'

We won the third Test at Lahore by nine wickets to complete a clean sweep, somewhat humiliating for the Aussies. Do you know, it was only the second time this century that the Australians have lost every match in a Test series? The South Africans over-ran them before in 1969–70.

Century of Centuries

It seemed odd and rather sad to me that we'd met India only 25 times since 1952. Blame politics for that. Now relations were cordial again and we intended wasting no time in offsetting their successes against us two years before. The weather in Lahore was less amiable. It was raining when we flew in, the wickets were covered by tarpaulin and the chances of serious net practice were minimal. Both teams delayed naming their side for the opening match. In the end Pakistan took the field without any semblance of spin. Gavaskar, who himself was only four Test centuries short of Sir Don Bradman's world record of 29, put us in to bat. And I was 25 not out overnight.

The match had a particular significance for me. A few days earlier I'd captained the Patron's XI against India and scored my 99th century. Now this was it. A Test match was surely as good an occasion as any; I'm not completely without a sense of the theatre.

For a reason I can't analyse I was never in any doubt about it. In a Stadium, which lacked atmosphere because there were so few spectators, I scored 215. It took me five and a half hours. There were 23 fours and two sixes. So much for figures; I was more eleated by the illustrious company I was now keeping. Here I was standing alongside Hobbs and Hendren and Hammond, Compton, Sutcliffe and Woolley. There were nineteen of them, I had been told, and now there were three of us—Sir Don and Glenn Turner were the others—who weren't British.

I went on the radio, talking in two tongues but saying basically the same thing. The bowling had been of a consistently good line; the wicket hadn't been difficult; there was no undue pressure because I was approaching a personal landmark. There had been one chance to third slip. We hadn't been scoring for several overs and I went for a cheeky single. I was angry with myself and there were no more lapses like that.

I phoned my parents. 'Well done, son,' they said as one. Najma was equally thrilled. So were the rest of the Pakistan players. Imran had told me he wouldn't be declaring and to just keep scoring. With that I revised my target and aimed for a double century instead. 'Nice one, Zed,' said Dilip Doshi, a friend of mine from county cricket days in England. I remembered his five wickets and almost as an afterthought grinned: 'You didn't do so badly yourself.' He shot back a roguish look which implied: 'I thought you'd forgotten!'

As a family we have many friends in Lahore: businessmen, landowners, farmers. They are always wonderfully hospitable and there was a series of parties given in my honour. Telegrams and messages of congratulations arrived for me, one from Bert Avery and Grahame Parker back in the West Country.

I had clearly given Imran the taste for more records himself. When we moved to Karachi for the second Test, there was a devastating defeat by an innings and 86 runs for India. They had never before gone down so badly against us; they had certainly never faced such movement as our captain produced in the second innings. He was virtually unplayable at times and the middle and late-order batsmen didn't relish the experience. Imran, with an imperious dominance that carried the rightful arrogance of authority, took 8–60 in just over 20 overs. Three of the late wickets came in seven balls.

The whole Pakistan team seemed to be looking for personal heights. Mohsin Khan had just before completed his third century in a row during a Test match at Lahore, and had passed 1,000 runs in a calendar year. Now Imran had taken his 200th Test wicket and India's manager, Rao Gaekwad was saying he'd never before seen such pace bowling, anywhere in the world. Sunil Gavaskar, no mean bowler himself—indeed his sole Test success in that role was at my expense!—was impishly implying, in a news interview, that it might be advisable to place a sightscreen between his batsmen and the Pakistan bowler in future matches.

Next stop Faisalabad. India were feeling pretty demoralised by this time and, off field friendships apart, we were in no especial mood for cricketing compromise. Four of us, one after the other, Javed, myself, Salim Malik and Imran scored punishing centuries. Javed and myself beat our own record for a fourth wicket stand against the Indians (287). My diligent young brother gave my memory a timely prod and I realised I was now Pakistan's highest scoring Test batsman; I had passed Majid's total.

It was a placid wicket and we should have felt sorry for the Indian bowlers. Kapil Dev, Maninder Singh (who toiled so hard for his first Test wicket and at least got Imran) and Doshi all conceded more than 100 runs. I exchanged a meaningful look more than once with the spinners.

By this time I'd scored five consecutive centuries, two of them in one-day matches. From England there was talk of another contract offer on its way to me. The county's annual meeting was looming and friends had told me that one or two pointed pro-Zaheer statements were being contemplated.

I chuckled to myself and was in good humour as once more my nightly dreams were filled with runs. The only unhappiness, in fact, had been the news that Tom Hennessy, my 'White Daddy' back in Bristol, had died.

Pakistan didn't exactly need me in the fourth Test, at Hyderabad. Mudassar Nazar and Javed Miandad set a new world Test record with a third wicket stand of 451. The previous best was by Denis Compton and Bill Edrich against the South Africans at Lords in 1947. Our pair both scored double centuries. For most of the time I remained padded-up, wishing fervently that I was out there, too. In the end I just about had time to stroke 25 not out, before we declared at 581 for three. I'm told that when Mudassar was out for 231, he and Javed needed just one more run to beat the Ponsford-Bradman record for ANY wicket in a Test match.

Remembering my problems and anxieties in England six months earlier, I was reassured by what was happening at home.

With his 'White Mummy and Daddy', Edna and the late Tom Hennessy, in Bristol.

Zaheer, with David Foot.

If, as they say, cricket is played with the mind as much as the body, I knew that the crease belonged to me. There were three one-day hundreds in a row for me and, yes, crowd trouble at Karachi in one of them. Students had been threatening to disrupt the game but I don't think they were behind the mindless hooliganism that held up play. There were 45,000 spectators and I suspect that most of them wanted to watch a cricket match.

I shall remember for a long time the way our skipper pulled up a stump and warded off trouble-makers who appeared to be making for Gavaskar, one of the batsmen at the time.

That's the ugly face of international cricket—and I'm only pained that Karachi has too often been the setting.

Mob law will not, I am determined, have the last word in this book. This has been my very personal story: a tale of a slim, introvert, studious-looking Sialkot boy's emergence as an international cricketer and history-maker.

No-one, I promise you, has ever derived greater pleasure or fulfillment from scoring runs. If that has become something of a repetitive and boring theme, I apologise. It is ME—my whole philosophy towards cricket. It has stirred, stimulated and fashioned me. Long ago I discovered to my joy that my main skill in life was making runs on a cricket field. I complemented that skill with my unshakable belief that batting can be a thing of beauty. I get no satisfaction from a hideous stroke, even when the ball reaches the boundary.

My intention is to go on scoring runs and centuries as attractively as possible. All I ask is that no-one in the process calls me a run machine. My cricket, around the world, is far too human an activity for that. I hope I've conveyed that humanity—the family support, the friendship, the little shafts of humour all the way from Hyderabad to Harrogate—beneath the sheer statistics of my career.

Career Feats

- At the end of the series against India early in 1983, Zaheer had played in 58 Test matches. His figures were:
  94 innings 7 not out 4,073 runs H.S. 274 Av 46.81
  There had been 11 Test centuries. He became Pakistan's highest scorer in Test matches during the third Test against India at Faisalabad in January 1983. Playing in his 55th Test, he beat Majid Khan's record of 3,931 runs. Zaheer actually scored five consecutive hundreds in that series, two of them in one-day matches and a century in the first three Tests.

- His first-class career record as he started the 1983 season in England was:
  663 innings 81 n.o. 31,440 runs H.S. 274 Av 54.02 (102 centuries)
  Eight times Zaheer has scored two centuries in match. On the last occasion, at Karachi in 1982, he beat Wally Hammond's world record.

- Playing for Gloucestershire in 1976 he twice scored a double century and a century in the same match—without being dismissed. Against Surrey at the Oval, he made 216no and 156no; against Kent at Canterbury, he made 230no and 104no. In 1977, against Sussex at Cheltenham, he scored 205no and 108no. This remarkable pattern was continued in 1981 when, against Somerset at Bath, he scored 215no and 150no.

- In the 1982–83 series against India, he became the first batsman to make more than 150 in three consecutive Test innings. His scores: 215, 186 and 168.

- He is only the second batsman in the history of the game to score his 100th century in a Test match. Geoffrey Boycott was the other, at Headingley in 1977, against Australia.

One Hundred Memories

Zaheer scored his 100th century at Lahore on 11 December 1982. In the process he became the 20th player to achieve this feat and only the third non-Englishman. Below is a comprehensive list of his 'century of first-class centuries'.

1.	19	Karachi v East Pakistan	(Karachi)	1968–69
2.	103*	Pakistan International Airlines v Bahawalpur	(Bahawalpur)	1969–70
3.	136*	Pakistan International Airlines v Karachi B	(Karachi)	1969–70
4.	136	Pakistan International Airlines v Karachi A	(Karachi)	1969–70
5.	118	Pakistan International Airlines A v East Pakistan Greens	(Dacca)	1970–71
6.	196	Pakistan International Airlines A v East Pakistan Whites	(Dacca)	1970–71
7.	161	Pakistan International Airlines A v Bahawalpur	(Karachi)	1970–71
8.	111	Pakistan International Airlines A v Punjab University	(Lahore)	1970–71
9.	202	Pakistan International Airlines A v Karachi Blues	(Karachi)	1970–71
10.	110	Pakistanis v Worcestershire	(Worcester)	1971
11.	138	Pakistanis v Kent	(Gravesend)	1971
12.	274	Pakistan v England	(Birmingham)	1971
13.	100*	Pakistanis v. Lancashire	(Manchester)	1971
14.	112	World XI v Western Australia	(Perth)	1971–72
15.	106	World XI v Tasmania Combined XI	(Hobart)	1971–72
16.	143	Pakistanis v Western Australia	(Perth)	1972–73
17.	113	Pakistanis v Tasmania	(Hobart)	1972–73
18.	105	Pakistanis v Central Districts	(Waganui)	1972–73
19.	170	Parkistanis v Wellington	(Wellington)	1972–73
20.	110	Pakistan International Airlines v Karachi	(Karachi)	1972–73
21.	153*	Gloucestershire v Surrey	(The Oval)	1973
22.	103	Gloucestershire v Somerset	(Bristol)	1973
23.	145	Pakistan XI v World XI	(Karachi)	1973–74
24.	129	Pakistan XI v World XI	(Lahore)	1973–74
25.	112	Pakistan International Airlines v Pakistan Railways	(Lahore)	1973–74
26.	112	Pakistan International Airlines v Punjab	(Lahore)	1973–74
27.	174	Pakistan International Airlines v Sind	(Lahore)	1973–74
28.	112	Gloucestershire v Cambridge University	(Cambridge)	1974
29.	137	Pakistanis v Minor Counties	(Jesmond)	1974
30.	104	Pakistanis v Glamorgan	(Swansea)	1974
31.	240	Pakistan v England	(The Oval)	1974
32.	117	Pakistanis v Sussex	(Hove)	1974
33.	131	Pakistan International Airlines v Pakistan Railways	(Lahore)	1974–75
34.	157	Pakistan International Airlines v National Bank	(Lahore)	1974–75
35.	111	Gloucestershire v Kent	(Cheltenham)	1975
36.	123	Gloucestershire v Nottinghamshire	(Nottingham)	1975
37.	170	Dawood Industries v Pakistan International Airlines	(Lahore)	1975–76
38.	155	Sind A v Pakistan Universities	(Lahore)	1975–76
39.	188	Gloucestershire v Yorkshire	(Leeds)	1976
40.	141	Gloucestershire v Somerset	(Taunton)	1976
41.	216*	Gloucestershire v Surrey	(The Oval)	1976
42.	156*			

No.	Score	Match	Venue	Year
43.	104	Gloucestershire v Sussex	(Gloucester)	1976
44.	153	Gloucestershire v Essex	(Cheltenham)	1976
45.	177	Gloucestershire v Glamorgan	(Cardiff)	1976
46.	177	Gloucestershire v Leicestershire	(Leicester)	1976
47.	230*	Gloucestershire v Kent	(Canterbury)	1976
48.	104*			
49.	106	Gloucestershire v Worcestershire		1976
50.	101	Pakistan v Australia	(Adelaide)1976–77	
51.	104	Gloucestershire v Sussex	(Hove)	1977
52.	105	Gloucestershire v Somerset	(Bristol)	1977
53.	205*	Gloucestershire v Sussex	(Cheltenham)	1977
54.	108*			
55.	100*	Gloucestershire v Hampshire	(Southampton)	1977
56.	100	Gloucestershire v Cambridge University	(Cambridge)	1978
57.	140	Gloucestershire v Somerset	(Taunton)	1978
58.	213	Gloucestershire v Sussex	(Hove)	1978
59.	104	Gloucestershire v Derbyshire	(Gloucester)	1978
60.	121	Gloucestershire v New Zealanders	(Bristol)	1978
61.	132	Gloucestershire v Hampshire	(Basingstoke)	1978
62.	176	Pakistan v India	(Faisalabad)	1978–79
63.	235*	Pakistan v India	(Lahore)	1978–79
64.	135	Pakistan v New Zealand	(Auckland)	1978–79
65.	126	Pakistan v South Australia	(Adelaide)	1978–79
66.	101	Gloucestershire v Glamorgan	(Cardiff)	1979
67.	147	Gloucestershire v Somerset	(Taunton)	1979
68.	151*	Gloucestershire v Warwickshire	(Brisbane)	1979
69.	111	Pakistan International Airlines v Lahore	(Lahore)	1979–80
70.	170	Pakistan International Airlines v Pakistan Railways	(Lahore)	1979–80
71.	114	Pakistanis v West Zone	(Pune)	1979–80
72.	104	Gloucestershire v Northamptonshire	(Bristol)	1980
73.	173	Gloucestershire v Somerset	(Taunton)	1980
74.	110*	Pakistan International Airlines v Karachi	(Karachi)	1980–81
75.	138	Pakistan International Airlines v Muslim Commercial Bank	(Karachi)	1980–81
76.	154*	Pakistan International Airlines v National Bank	(Lahore)	1980–81
77.	100*	Pakistan International Airlines v Pakistan Railways	(Lahore)	1980–81
78.	100*			
79.	215*	Gloucestershire v Somerset ·	(Bath)	1981
80.	150*			
81.	101*	Gloucestershire v Hampshire	(Southampton)	1981
82.	100	Gloucestershire v Warwickshire	(Gloucester)	1981
83.	135*	Gloucestershire v Northamptonshire	(Northamptonshire)	1981
84.	128			
85.	145	Gloucestershire v Sussex	(Hove)	1981
86.	159	Gloucestershire v Glamorgan	(Bristol)	1981
87.	136*	Gloucestershire v Kent	(Cheltenham)	1981
88.	103*	Gloucestershire v Worcestershire	(Worcester)	1981
89.	117	Pakistanis v South Australia	(Adelaide)	1981–82
90.	134	Pakistan v Sri Lanka	(Lahore)	1981–82
91.	144	Gloucestershire v Oxford University	(Oxford)	1982
92.	162*	Gloucestershire v Lancashire	(Gloucester)	1982
93.	107			
94.	147	Pakistanis v Worcestershire	(Worcester)	1982
95.	148*	Pakistanis v Derbyshire	(Chesterfield)	1982
96.	126	Pakistan v Australia	(Faisalabad)	1982–83
97.	125	Pakistan International Airlines v Karachi	(Karachi)	1982–83
98.	101			
99.	108	BCCP Patron's XI v Indians	(Rawalpindi)	1982–83
100.	215	Pakistan v India	(Lahore)	1982–83

*Not out

(With acknowledgement to Brian Heald and *The Cricketer* Quarterly Facts and Figures).

BIBLIOGRAPHY

T. Bailey HISTORY OF CRICKET. Allen & Unwin, 1978.

B. Brain ANOTHER DAY, ANOTHER MATCH. Allen & Unwin, 1981.

R. Marlar THE STORY OF CRICKET. Marshall Cavendish, 1979.

Ray Robinson THE WILDEST TESTS. Pelham, 1972.

R. G. D. Willis CRICKET REVOLUTION. Sidgewick & Jackson, 1981.

Wisden Cricketers' Almanack—various years. Macdonald & Co.

Periodicals
The Cricketer International
The Cricket Quarterly Facts & Figures
Wisden Cricket Monthly
Year Books of Gloucestershire C.C.C.

INDEX

155